GW00400049

HEARTFELT

For Rhonda
You deepen me daily

For Keith
Never forget this happened

Heartfelt

*Finding Our Way
Back to God*

Gerrit Scott Dawson

The Bible Reading Fellowship
OPENING THE BIBLE

Text copyright © 1993 Gerrit Scott Dawson

First published by Upper Room Books,
Nashville, Tennessee, USA.

The author asserts the moral right to be
identified as the author of this work.

This edition published by
The Bible Reading Fellowship
Peter's Way, Sandy Lane West
Oxford OX4 5HG
ISBN 0 7459 3080 8

This edition 1996
10 9 8 7 6 5 4 3 2 1 0

Acknowledgments
Unless otherwise stated, scripture is taken
from the New Revised Standard Version
of the Bible copyright © 1989 by the
Division of Christian Education of the National
Council of the Churches of Christ in the USA.

Scripture marked (NIV) is taken from the Holy
Bible, New International Version. Copyright ©
1973, 1978, 1984 International Bible Society. By
permission of Hodder and Stoughton Ltd.

Scripture marked (KJV) is from the Authorized
Version of the Bible (The King James Bible), the
rights of which are vested in the Crown, and is
reproduced by permission of the Crown's Patentee,
Cambridge University Press.

A catalogue record for this book is
available from the British Library

Printed and bound in Great Britain
by Cox and Wyman Ltd, Reading

Contents

Introduction

THIS BOOK IS FOR PEOPLE WHO ARE LOOKING FOR A stronger connection with God. I have in mind those who are familiar with Christianity but who feel that their experience of traditional faith has not been enough for them. Perhaps a fresh approach to relating to Jesus as we find him in the Gospels would be helpful. If we could tunnel under the wall which has blocked us from God, we might be able to open the channel for a vital spiritual energy to flow into our lives.

I hear from many people who feel far from God. There are a variety of barriers they experience. Sometimes the sense of separation is very vague. I know a woman, for example, who has lived her life trying to do the right things. She has loved her family, worked hard, attended church, and served in the Sunday school. And yet, every now and then she has been overcome with sadness. She has grown lonely for something she cannot name. She has groped for it but felt thwarted in her search.

A brief but serious medical complication opened up the clogged passageways for a time. In the most precarious moments, the woman felt loved and protected to the depths of her being. She realized that her longing has been for God. After the crisis she began to pursue spiritual growth, but the old blocks rose up again. All the words of faith swirled in her head and seemed to make no sense. She wanted to find a way back to God.

I am thinking also of a man who has felt cut off from Christian faith because of an experience he had with the church. At an early age, the church was an agent not of love but of judgment, first towards one of his parents, then towards him. It always seemed as if he was on the discard pile of church priority; they didn't need him. There were so many others who fitted in better.

And so today he feels blocked from a deep relationship with God. If pressed, he would say that of course he loves God; he likes to be near religious services. He appreciates worship and study groups, but ultimately he feels on the outside looking in.

Because a life of spiritual depth has seemed unavailable to him, he has chosen to occupy his thoughts with making his way successfully in the world. With great energy, he has pursued the prizes and diversions of financial achievement. And for the most part that quest has sufficiently occupied his thoughts. He has had fun and has felt reasonably satisfied. But we all know how the story goes. The longer he succeeds, the less of a consuming challenge his work life will become, and the more space there will be inside him for a very old yearning to start moving around. He will have a spiritual ache but will not know how to find relief.

I am thinking as well of a woman who never felt adequate, though she had, to outside eyes, every gift one could want. She was attractive and keen, with parents who loved her and provided for her. Perhaps she had too much. From as early as she could remember, she wanted to prove that she deserved what she had. So she drove herself toward perfection and failed every time. She drank to escape the feeling of shame, and woke up to feel still more shame. Eventually she bottomed out and sought help.

Through the miraculous fellowship of Twelve Step groups[1], she became sober and began to deal honestly with her life. Then she discovered that she wanted something more. She told me this, 'My best friend in recovery has gotten very religious. She asks me to church, and I go with her. Every time we sing hymns I know, I start to cry. At first I didn't know why. Now I think it's because they remind me of home. And I want to be there. Not physically home, but spiritually. My problem, though, is that I'm not sure if I'm a Christian any more. Christian faith was given to me in my girlhood, but what about now? I don't know if I believe in Jesus. But I want to.'

There are many others. Some have a deep rift with God, created by some kind of terrible loss, which needs to be gently healed. Some simply desire to take a healthy faith deeper and are looking for fresh ways to do it. Some have nagging doubts which they would like to have addressed from a different view. For all kinds of reasons, then, many people are longing for a deeper connection to God than they have previously found in the church.

I believe passionately that such a relationship can be developed as we meet Jesus in the Gospels. In this book I will invite you to 'try on' the idea that Jesus still speaks, still lives, still engages people who encounter him. Working with this assumption, if only imaginatively, we will explore such questions as: What does Jesus offer? What does he want from me? What will happen if I follow him?

We will be working with ten stories of Jesus. My hope is that you will be able to find yourself in the characters of these narratives. If we can hook up our lives with their lives for a while, it just might be possible that we can be moved, healed, transformed, and invigorated, as they were.

Reading is usually a solitary endeavour. I hope my comments on these stories will help to open up your inner life during your personal reflections. This type of Bible study, though, can be even more effective if done in groups. When we engage in these stories with others, many more meanings and possibilities surface. There are questions and exercises at the end of each chapter that can be used for group study. I invite you to find another person or two who might be interested in plumbing the depths of these Gospel stories with you. Most of all, I wish you a vivid encounter with Jesus that leads you to feel connected to God in a wonderful way.

Notes

[1] Twelve Step groups are those such as Alcoholics Anonymous.

A note on footnotes

At the end of each chapter, the author sometimes notes publications he has referred to in the text. These are often for the US edition of a book which is not always available in the UK.

~1~

Watching Down the Foreign Road

W E BEGIN WITH A STORY NOT ABOUT JESUS, BUT one he told about two brothers and their father. I hesitate to bring the story of the Prodigal Son into this first chapter. Nearly everyone who has spent any time around Christianity has heard it. To consider reading about it may evoke, 'Oh, but I already know that one. Can you tell me something new?' Hopefully, though, working with the story of the Prodigal Son will be more like watching a favourite movie again. Before it comes on, I think I am not too interested. I probably would not *choose* to watch this movie tonight. But if I watch it for just a moment, then I'm hooked all over again.

This story is the third in a series Jesus told about the ways God looks for us when we are lost and far from home. Jesus said, 'There was a man who had two sons. The younger of them said to his father: "Father, give me the share of the property that will belong to me." So, he divided his property between them. A few days later the younger son gathered all he had and travelled to a distant country, and there he squandered his property in dissolute living.'

The younger son left home. Perhaps this was just part of normal growing up. We cannot be children for ever; at some point we have to make our own way. But this man left by burning his bridges. According to the custom of the day, asking for his inheritance while his father still lived was like saying, 'Father, I wish you were already dead.' The son repudiated his heritage. He disgraced his family. He left all that he had ever been or had been taught.[1]

The turning point in the story occurs after his money had run out and an economic depression hit the country. The young man took a job slopping pigs and grew so hungry that even those pig pods looked appetizing. His need became desperate. And then, as Jesus told the story, the son 'came to himself'. He 'came to'; he woke up. This wonderfully succinct phrase implies that somehow the man had gone away from himself. He had started on a course of life and could not stop until he ran out of resources. To use other words, he 'bottomed out'. And then he woke up.

Sometimes, without even knowing it, we get ourselves on a road away from ourselves and God. We may not even know how far away we are until the money runs out and our stomachs growl with hunger. These pangs we experience vary in intensity. We may feel vaguely that life is just not what we thought it would be. We had always planned for something different. Or we may feel sharply dissatisfied; we may wake up with an awful sense of self-loathing. We may feel the years have been wasted and so little love has been shared. Whatever the intensity level, we realize when we wake up that we are away from home.

At first we may not be able to describe home; we simply know we are not there. We may not know in those waking moments what being ourselves is supposed to be; but we feel sure that we have not been living in harmony with our innermost design. We may not have a description for what connecting with God could be like; we realize, however, that we are a long way from such a connection. Our need yanks us awake, we discover how far we are from home, and we begin to search for a way to get back.

In Jesus' story, the father who lets the son go clearly represents God. Somehow, then, God is intimately connected with all that makes up home. The father in the story is the source of blessing; his house is the place where life is in balance. On his land is to be found the work that satisfies and generates an abundant harvest.

The younger son left that home, pillaging part of its wealth, to live in his own way. When we leave being who we most truly are, we leave God. God is not alien to us; God is within the inmost part of us. If we would be at peace and at home with ourselves, we will have to be at home with God.

The Impulse to Leave

Who knows why we go away? Some say they went because they wanted to try their hand at the world's game. Our culture prizes the achievements of position and wealth. Such rewards entice us to try and master the game, even at risk to our sense of self.

Some went in quest of the mysterious, to seek the rush of experience or the passion of the arts. Those of a religious temperament may have left all they knew of God in search of God.

Others went off to fill up a sense of unworthiness with accomplishment in their chosen field. And it was not enough. Imperfections had to be hidden; thoughts of what was being sacrificed had to be quelled. Some left the home of their deepest selves as they simply tried to fill the expectations others had for them. One may have leaped into a marriage without reflection and then tried awfully hard to live a particular appearance. Another may have pursued someone else's measure of a successful life.

Some of us left home because we deliberately closed off our connection to God. Perhaps an experience of rejection in the church led us to pack our bags and leave anything religious. Some have been caught in legalistic beliefs that sucked the life out of them. There was no way to reason out of that trap, so they simply left faith behind. Still another may have given up trying to relate to God because of suffering a loss so searing that bitterness has continued to block any possibility of faith.

There are thousands of reasons which sent us away from home. They may have begun in a conflict with God or with a division inside ourselves. Either way, the result is the same. We are in a foreign land, and the money is running out. The roads we took and our reasons for leaving can get lost in the past. We only know that today we feel far from home.

The poet George Herbert knew well our urge to leave home and strike out on our own. He understood how our defiance can grow when we think there is something better for us in another place. In 'The Collar', the poet expresses how he feels trapped by the expectations of his faith about what is right. So he pounds the table and attempts to declare his independence. He is going to get what we wants before life passes him by, instead of wasting his life at home. Herbert writes,

> I struck the board, and cried, 'No more!
> I will abroad.
> What? shall I ever sigh and pine?
> My lines and life are free; free as the road,
> Loose as the wind, as large as store.
> . . . .
> Sure there was wine
> Before my sighs did dry it: there was corn
> Before my tears did drown it.
> Is the year only lost to me?
> Have I no bays to crown it?
> No flowers, no garlands gay? All blasted?
> All wasted?
> Not so, my heart: but there is fruit,
> And thou hast hands.

Herbert hit the nerve of our impulse to wander. Something in many of us makes a bold declaration: 'My life is free, free as the road, loose as the wind.' I can live how I want to live, for my life is my own. There is fruit to be tasted in the world, and I have hands to pluck it down. I am going after it. Quietly or with a flash, brazenly or almost imperceptibly, many of us have taken a road away from our heart's home.

When the son had come to himself, his pride was broken, and he determined to go back to his father and ask for a job as a servant. The young man felt shame, but his need was stronger than his guilt. He prepared a speech of confession. 'Father, I have sinned against heaven and before you; I am no longer worthy to be called your son; treat me like one of your hired servants.' The younger son hoped at best to be taken on as a hired hand.

Jesus continued, 'But while he was still far off, his father saw him and was filled with compassion; he ran and put his arms around him and kissed him.' The son tried to make his speech, but the father would not listen. He called for a robe and a ring, and a great celebration. 'For this son of mine was dead and is alive again; he was lost and is found!'

The father had been watching down the road for his son. The son had shamed him; by custom the father could have repudiated the very existence of such a wanton child. Wasting time looking for his return made the father subject to derision. But the father was crazy about his son; he loved him enough to cast his sight down the foreign road every day his child was away. When his son returned, he showered the shame with a welcome.

What would it mean to learn that someone is watching with straining eyes down the road to catch a glimpse of you? When we are far from home, what would happen if we realized that someone was waiting for the first signs of our return from a foreign land, waiting to celebrate our first steps home with open arms and a banquet of celebration?

In the epilogue of Dostoyevsky's novel, *Crime and Punishment*, we read of the beginning of renewal for the story's main character, Raskolnikov. Towards the beginning of the story, Raskolnikov had murdered an old woman pawnbroker, feeling no remorse and justifying his act as ridding society of an undesirable. Throughout the epic, he was wholly absorbed in himself—a narcissist fit for the twentieth century.

Although Raskolnikov is certainly an unattractive character, one woman loved him all along. Sonia even followed Raskolnikov all the way to the Siberian work camp where he was sentenced to seven years of hard labour for his crime. She came to the fence every day to speak with him during their brief breaks in the work.

For a long time Raskolnikov spurned her presence. It meant nothing to him. He would remain quiet when he was with her, as if annoyed. Then Raskolnikov fell ill and was placed in the hospital ward for many weeks.

Sonia tried to see him but only rarely could gain admittance. Still, she came every day, 'sometimes only to stand a minute and look up at the windows of the ward.'

Raskolnikov's condition improved slowly. One evening he felt strong enough to rise from his bed and go to the window. He looked out and saw Sonia standing at the hospital gate; she appeared to be waiting for something. 'Something stabbed him to the heart at that minute.' He realized that every day he had been ill, unable to rise, believing himself alone in his misery, Sonia had come to the gate to wait awhile for him.

Raskolnikov looked for Sonia eagerly the next day. But she did not come. Nor the next day. And then Raskolnikov understood that he was waiting for Sonia. Before, Sonia had been the one waiting; now he was waiting for Sonia. Before it had made no difference to him, but now he was expecting her. Before he loathed her; now he discovered that as he waited for her, he loved her.

When they met again at last, Raskolnikov found that 'all at once something seemed to seize him and fling him at her feet. He wept and threw his arms around her knees.' Sonia had outwaited his self-absorption until love broke through him at last. The one so far from home, in Siberia and detached from his own soul, finally understood that someone had waited for him every day. He reconnected to life and came home to himself.[2]

There is one who waits for us. He stands every day in the yard looking up at the ward where we lie on a bed, mired in thoughts of our condition. He comes every day and stands in the cold winter light, and he waits while we think life is only this sick bed and the wants of our illness. He waits in the yard for the evening when we get up and look out of the window and see him there, and our hearts are stabbed. Someone is waiting for me to come home! Our shame will not be answered with recrimination, but with tender forgiveness. He has not waited begrudgingly; he is not angry. This loving one has let go all the time that has gone by. He just wants us in his arms.

The father strained his eyes down the foreign road for any sign of his son. The boy didn't know that, of course. He didn't really think of his father until he was so hungry that pride was impossible. Then he got up and started home.

We can wait that long if we like. The trouble is we may not get so abjectly hungry that we have no choice until many years have passed. But if we were to step into this story Jesus told and begin to consider that the father is waiting for us now, would that be enough to get us to our feet?

We may be able to slop the pigs for a long

time, if we do not believe there is any other choice, if shame prevents thoughts of home. But what yearning homeward is awakened when we discover that there is one who waits for us, watching every day for any sign of our return, ready to embrace us even in our filth, to love us through the shame!

George Herbert concluded his poem of rebellion with these words,

> But as I raved and grew more fierce and wild
> At every word,
> Methoughts I heard one calling, *Child!*
> And I replied, *My Lord.*

There are so many of us who feel as if we are far away from something we need to be close to. The emotion is very nebulous. And often if someone tries to diagnose us with precision, to say, 'What you need is . . . ' we close it off. What we are missing is so important to us that instinctively we close out superficial explanations. We have come to ourselves enough to know that we need to start toward home. But we may not be sure in which direction to begin. We may not be at all convinced anyone will welcome us when we arrive. The rest of this book is for those who feel the urge to get up and start down the road towards home.

Questions for Reflection or Discussion

The story of the younger son is found in Luke 15:11–24.

1) What drives us to seize the inheritance, liquidate it, and strike out for a foreign country?

2) In what ways do you feel you have left home, in the sense that you feel away from your deepest self, away from God?

3) What feelings are evoked in you by the picture of the father watching with strained eyes down the road for signs of your return?

4) What resistance will you need to overcome before starting towards home?

Exercises

1) Jot down some words that describe the personality of the younger son; write some words that express his condition after the money runs out. Then, make a list of words that come to mind when you think of the young man's father.

2) Imagine that you are the younger son (or daughter, if that makes it easier), longing to return.

Prepare your homecoming speech. Allow your paragraph to be a reflection on your life and any ways in which you feel far from home.

3) Write a conversation between yourself as the younger child and the father who has waited for your return. Carry the story further by imagining what you talk about on the way back to the house. As the child, what feels important to say? How does the longsuffering parent, who is God, answer your concerns? Be sure to conclude your conversation with the father's words, 'For this son (daughter) of mine was dead and is alive again; he (she) was lost and is found!'

4) The lines quoted above from George Herbert work well as a prayer.

Notes

[1] A wonderful commentary on how Jesus' audience would have understood this story is found in Thomas E. Boomershine, *Story Journey*, Abingdon Press, Nashville, 1988.

[2] With thanks to W. H. Vanstone for his commentary on this work in *The Stature of Waiting*.

~2~

When Being Good Isn't Enough

NOT EVERYONE GOES AWAY LIKE THE YOUNGER brother. Some of us stay at home and dutifully take care of responsibilities. We have not had any major breaks with the values we received as children. Our parents rarely worried about us late at night. For the most part we have maintained our faith in God, perhaps even serving in the church as part of our civic responsibility. Communities are built upon such people. Churches make pillars out of those who are like the older brother in Jesus' story.

When the younger son returned home, the father called for a feast. Almost immediately there was music and dancing in the house. But there was still time left in the work day. The young man's older brother was out in the fields tending to the farm. As he got near the house, he heard the merriment and wondered what was going on. He asked a servant boy and was told, 'Your brother has come, and your father has killed the fatted calf, because he has got him back safe and sound.' As he thought about this, the older brother got so angry that he refused to go to the party.

Shortly, his father came out and pleaded with his son. But it did no good. The young man replied, 'Listen! For all these years I have been working like a slave for you, and I have never disobeyed your command; yet you have never given me even a young goat so that I might celebrate with my friends. But when this son of yours came back, who has devoured your property with prostitutes, you killed the fatted calf for him!'

In the course of an hour, the father had gained one son but had nearly lost the other one. Suddenly it seemed that a happy, normal life had been all along a life of drudgery. Was this what it meant all these years? The older brother perceived his life as working like a slave, obeying orders, slogging through each day in unexpressed hopes of some reward of distracting entertainment. He lived with his father, and was yet as far away as a foreigner.

An Absence of Joy

The older brother's sudden declaration of estrangement was extreme. In varying degrees of intensity, though, a number of us may experience this kind of distance from God. One common quality our faith may have with the older son is a dearth of joy.

We find, perhaps, that we have no particular antipathy towards God; we simply have trouble getting deeper than the surface of religious practice. Some worry that although they go to church, say their prayers, and try to live a good life, their faith stays small and their experience of God is negligible. Persisting in us is a quiet sense that, while others can connect with God, we do not. Others are acting like they get it, and we may look like them; yet we feel that through some fault of ours, spiritual life is simply not vital.

Further, like the older brother, our resentment can build when our sense of duty blocks our connection to the joy that underlies all the work. If we pray without any experience of the presence of God, before long the activity is empty habit. Going to church regularly becomes drudgery when appearance before others replaces warm fellowship. We can burn out on social service when there is no underlying spring replenishing our energies. It is no fun at all to check our impulses and live a self-controlled, moral life if we have no sense of being part of a higher purpose by doing so. Religion can become a chore. God is one more burden in a life of requirements. We do our service but hope that nothing more will be asked.

In that state, an inner loneliness may prevail. The yearning to be with the father, in whose fields we plough, in whose presence we are so close, occasionally makes us want to get up and go into his room and talk. But we are not sure that we have earned the right. Such direct contact would be too unsettling. Instead, we labour on, speak politely to him at the proper times, but realize little joy in the relationship or in the heritage of our faith. Compromises are made to keep sharp edges away. 'You can't go by everything you read in the Bible,' we catch ourselves saying. 'Some people are just more religious than others; they seem to get it more than we ordinary churchgoers.'

Too Much Responsibility

Another sentiment we may share with the older brother is a feeling of bondage to responsibilities. The younger brother left without a thought towards how the family would get along maintaining the estate in his absence. The older son, though, never entertained thoughts of leaving for long. He knew that he was needed, and he lived in service to duty.

One child leaves town, makes her own way, gets married, and raises a family miles from home. Another child stays nearby and tends the family heritage. When the parents grow ill, the child at home takes on the burden. He feels he has no choice and, in fact, wouldn't want an alternative. But how it burns when that spendthrift sister can hardly manage a week away to lend a hand!

Children who grow up in alcoholic families may find the same struggle, magnified to disastrous dimensions. One child seems to bear the weight of the family in her own body. It's her fault that Mum and Dad fight. Her father drinks because she, the unexpected, unwanted child was born. She spends her life trying to fix things, trying to take control of the uncontrollable, shovelling her life into the bottomless hole of her parent's addiction. Is it any wonder she gets migraines no doctor can explain? She is the one who cleans up her father, makes dinner, does the laundry, and becomes the family counsellor at age thirteen.

And how she hates her brother who seems unaffected by all this! This other child comes and goes as he wishes. He feels no compulsion to stay and fix things. It's not his fault; he won't buy into it. He's got his own life to live. And so he incurs the righteous indignation of the poor little one caught in a trap that has made her old before her time.

Some people simply have a stronger sense of responsibility than others. They take burdens upon themselves willingly. The needs of others always weigh upon them. Most of the time, this way of life is fine. But there are days when resentment builds—they carry so much while others seem to skate along: How can it be that other people find God so easily while I struggle every day to be faithful and get nowhere? How can that person just waltz in here after the rest of us have held things together for so long?

I experience the older brother's anger when I feel that everything depends on me and no one appreciates my obvious contributions to the maintenance of the cosmos. I begin to squirm over my toil. No one is helping me. Why do I have to slave away at this when no one cares? I might, for instance, serve my family this peevishness as I serve breakfast. My attitude says, 'Here's the food your loving father has made for you, you ungrateful wretches.' All the time I block the joy in my life.

I forget the love which I have for each of the children—the pleasure in preparing breakfast on a sunny morning, smelling coffee or feeling the cold in a glass of juice. All are lost on me then. I am tight, petty, breathless. Never mind the joy of being a child of God, forgiven and blessed by Christ. Those thoughts are miles away. I just want to get these jobs done, so I can be at peace. But of course it never works that way. Whether the task is as simple as making a meal or as serious as caring for an aged parent, those crushed by a sense of duty find the work never ends. The connection to joy, and to God, must be made at another level.

You Are Always with Me

We have said earlier that the father in the story is the source of a blessed life. His house is a celebration of abundance balanced with hard but satisfying work. To labour for this father is to live out one's full potential. There is joy in working his fields and contributing to his resources. In the midst of a famine, the father extends a generous hand offering food. The father is God, and his house is our deepest home.

The older brother was part of that vigorous house. But he lost his connection to the joy of its life. He could not find the reason for labouring to maintain it, and so it seemed to him a house of slavery.

The father replied to the son, 'Son you are always with me, and all that is mine is yours.' The father assumes that the son desires to be with him. I wonder if the older son had ever thought of that. This is a wonderful reversal. He doesn't say, 'I am always with you,' implying something about himself, as if he hovered around the son, restricting his freedom. Rather, '*You* are always with me.'

What did the young man think of that?

Perhaps he wanted to answer, 'No, I'm not. I'm out working in the fields most of the time. The sun is there, making me thirst, sapping my strength. But you spend the day looking down the road for my brother. I don't see you until the end of the day, and we rarely have much to say.'

Then the father might clarify, 'Look: you, my son, are right here, in my home, on our farm, doing our work. You are near me, you have access to me at all times. You can be with me whenever you want. I always have time for you, but I won't hound you while you are busy. I am always interested in what you are feeling and doing.'

The joy he desired he already possessed. Already he was always with the father. All he had to do was become aware of that reality and enjoy it. Jesus' story is telling those of us who are older brothers, frustrated and striving, that we are with God already. That is our status. God is not hovering over us to scowl when every duty is not perfectly completed. In all that we do, we are already with God. We may enjoy the house of blessing in which we already live.

What would it mean to you if God were to say, 'Daughter, son, you are always with me. It doesn't make any difference whether you are thinking of me; I am always thinking of you. I am keeping you with me.' Every moment, we are with

God. God is with us. All that is God's is ours. We are already connected. Such news is almost unbelievable. How can over-achievers not have to work for such joy?

'All That Is Mine Is Yours.'

The father also said, 'And all that is mine is yours.' I like to imagine the conversation which could have occurred when the older son began to think about this.

> **Son**: 'You mean I'm free? I could go off and spend all your money, and have parties and live away from home?'
> **Father**: 'Of course. That has always been an option.'
> **Son**: 'I could ask for anything I want and get it?'
> **Father**: 'Yes.'
> **Son**: 'I could quit, and the farm wouldn't fall into ruin?'
> **Father**: 'Of course not. It doesn't depend on you. You may contribute if you like and share in our harvest. But I have plenty of resources. You may go if you like. Do you want to leave your work and home now, like your brother?'

Son: 'Yes. Well, no. Actually, I like being responsible; I really have always liked being at home. I just get tired sometimes of all I have to do.'

Father: 'Leave the burden of the harvest to me. I'll see to that.'

Son: 'But don't you want me to do better? Aren't you going to tell me to earn my way?'

Father: 'Son, you are already with me. You already have all that I have. Now come in to the party. It's all right to celebrate. The work will keep. Your brother has just returned to his senses and come home. He was dead and is alive again. He is back with us. He was lost and is found.'

There is a lifting of a burden in the father's words. No more striving is needed. Right now, already, all that God has is ours. God is always with us. Our work, then, is the joy of contributing to God's work, the estate of blessing offered to the world. And though we labour, the harvest does not depend on us. God is the master of the house. Our joy is to be living as those who already belong and already share in the life of God. We can leave if we want to; God's land will still be ploughed; the harvest will still be reaped. We can take off if we desire. But we already know that deep down we don't want to go, particularly now that we know that God is responsible. We need not sweat to prove our worth anymore; we need not strive to get the inheritance. That is all done. It is all taken care of already.

Moving Ahead

When we feel distant from God, it may be that we have taken the foreign road away from ourselves or it may be that we have viewed our lives as duty without joy. Either way, Jesus' parable tells us that God stands ready to welcome us home. We are watched for down the road by a loving father. We are implored to come in and join the party. It is time to start down the road to home, to come in from the fields of duty to the party, and to meet one another over the love of the father. On the way, we learn that we have something to teach each other: some of us about going away, others about staying home. Together, we can learn what life is like labouring in the house of blessing.

Such an invitation has great appeal to me. Unfortunately, I realize that our spiritual lives unfold with a bit more complexity. After the initial joy of starting home, we will have some work to do. The old layers still need to be peeled away. The joy of discovering that we are with God and all God has is ours will fade soon if we do not continue to deal with the underlying issues.

Questions for Reflection or Discussion

The story of the older brother is found in Luke 15:25–32.

1) Make a list of the personality characteristics of the older brother. What does he live for?

2) When do you experience your life as constant responsibility?

3) What makes us resistant to the possibility that joy is so close at hand?

4) What reasons do you give for not going into the party?

5) Do you think the older brother went into the party after the talk with his father? What would have prevented him? What might have inspired him?

6) What would it mean to you to hear in the depths of you from God, 'Son, daughter, you are always with me, and all that is mine is yours'?

Exercises

1) Imagine that the older brother decides to go into the party; after a while he and the younger brother sit down together in a corner to discuss this return and their father.

   a) If you are working alone, write a dialogue between the two brothers which explores the new situation of one brother's return home and another brother's presence at the party. Explore what will be needed for reconciliation between the brothers and between each of them and their father. You may want to bring the father into the conversation at some point.

   b) If you are working in a group, play out the conversation in pairs, with one partner as the older brother, the other as the younger. For a twist, invite a third person to be the father. At first, he will sit silently, listening. Then, after a few minutes he could enter the conversation.

   Or, work the conversations in teams, one for the older brother, one for the younger. Both could list their needs, their feelings, their interest in the new life with the father. Then talk back and forth as a team.

2) Imagine that it is the next day. The older brother has been thinking about the conversation with his father and wishes now to take advantage of this new-found access. What does he say when he goes in to see his father? Write this conversation.

3) One way to enter these stories more fully is to use poems or prayers written by others. Their very newness to us may be a helpful way to experience the stories on a different level. Read this line from St. John of the Cross:

> My spirit has become dry because it forgets to feed on you.[1]

with these lines from a Gaelic prayer,

> I am serene because I know thou lovest me.
> Because thou lovest me, nought can move me from my peace.
> Because thou lovest me, I am as one to whom all good has come.[2]

Notes

[1] George Appleton, editor, *The Oxford Book of Prayer*, Oxford University Press, New York, 1985, page 139

[2] Ibid

~3~

Everything I Ever Did

IF IT WERE JUST AS SIMPLE AS TAKING THE FIRST STEPS, then reconnecting with God would not be such a problem for us. We have so many images for the beginning of the journey: going home, getting sober, being born again, going into the party, turning a new leaf. But once our yearning awakes us, and we get going, the underlying issues of our separation from God also arise. They demand our attention. God calls us to go deeper toward a resolution of anything that disconnects us. And that can produce a new resistance in us.

'Without knowledge of self there is no knowledge of God. . . . Without knowledge of God there is no knowledge of self.' So begins John Calvin's famous *Institutes of the Christian Religion*. There seems to be some interrelation between a growing awareness of God and an increased consciousness of our own lives. One leads to the other; the absence of one prevents the other. We cannot plumb the mystery of our being without knowledge of God. Just as surely, we get no farther in reconnecting with God if we are not willing to be led to a more honest exploration of what makes us who we are. Jesus was an expert at taking people deeper into themselves. He brought to light the hidden places and invited people to open themselves to God.

Once, in the region of Samaria, Jesus met a woman by a well at noontime. Their conversation was a steady spiral into the depths of the woman's life and a new understanding of God. In this story we learn quite a bit about the way Jesus dealt with people. This conversation can be a metaphor for many of us as well.

The Dailiness of Life

The Samaritans were considered by Jews to be traitorous, unclean half-breeds. Years before, the Jews in that region had intermarried with the Babylonian conquerors, rejected portions of the Hebrew scriptures, worshipped not in Jerusalem but on Mt Gerizim, and failed to support a Jewish uprising against the Romans. So, the Jews of Samaria had become Samaritans. No one is so hated as those most like us in all but a few crucial ways. The Jews considered the Samaritans unclean; contact with them was disdained.

Jesus passed through Samaria on his way

north and stopped by a well to rest. He saw a woman who had come to draw water. There was no one else around. The hour was noon, and no doubt it was hot in the blazing Middle Eastern sun. It was strange that she had come alone to a well outside the town at the hottest time of day. Usually the women came in the morning or the evening, and they came together for safety and companionship. There was some reason why this particular woman did not want the company of others.

She had come to perform the daily necessity of gathering fresh water. Every day there was the long walk out with the heavy earthen jar, then the drawing from the well, and the trip home with the full container weighing her down.

At the time of this story, the Samaritan woman was engaged in the day's obligation of a perpetual chore. Her labour was made harder by whatever reasons she had for coming alone at an off hour.

We know what it is to be caught in the dailiness of life and how our routine may be shaped by our own particular pain. There are the repetitive tasks, the constant requirements which can make one day blur into another, so that at the end of a year we may hardly remember where all the time went. We are pumping old water from the bottom of the world. And the pain in our lives is keeping us out of joint so habitually that we may even forget that it is not normal to draw water in the heat of the day. We may have lived without kind words for so long that we no longer expect them. The ache of a betrayal may have been with us until hollowness seems like a natural feeling. We may have borne the pain of separation in relationships for enough years that we have grown to rely upon it, as part of our daily rhythm.

An Interruption in the Routine

And then, one day, the Samaritan woman's routine was broken by the presence of a man at the well. Her guard went up. She knew about men. He asked for a drink. She sized him up and replied, 'How is it that you, a Jew, ask a drink of me, a woman of Samaria?' Jesus had broken the agreed bounds of conversation. Rabbis did not speak to women in public. Contemporary Jews avoided dealings with Samaritans; certainly, sharing a drinking vessel would have made one feel filthy.

Jesus had a habit of entering territory not assigned to him by traditional roles. We may well have feelings similar to the woman's: How can it be, Jesus, that you want something of me? I am not one of your saints. Churchy people may hang on your every word. But not me; it's doubtful that you will find in me something religious that you might need. I thought we agreed long ago that I wouldn't bother you if you wouldn't bother me.

Jesus countered by turning the discussion around. 'If you knew the gift of God and who it is that is saying to you, "Give me a drink," you would have asked him, and he would have given you living water.' The conversation switched from what she had to offer to the gift of God. Jesus tantalized her with the implication that what he had to give was highly desirable.

To enter such a conversation with Jesus would open an opportunity we yearn for, if only we could see it. Here is the possibility that there is a gift of God we may receive. God waits to give us something wonderful and important—something we ache for.

But the Samaritan woman was not so easily taken. Perhaps this was another line from yet another man. She looked him over again.

'Sir, you have no bucket, and the well is deep. Where do you get that living water? Are you greater than our ancestor Jacob, who gave us the well?' This stranger who broke social customs out in the hot sun had no visible means to give her any gift at all.

We might very well ask Jesus ourselves, 'Really now, what do you have to give me? Can you possibly have something that has anything to do with my daily life? You have no bucket, and the well is deep. You are not relevant to the complexities of the relationships I am in. You want it all black and white—a perfect fairy-tale marriage—and I am far away from that. You do not know about the pressures of my business. Ten people pull me from every direction. Surely you are just the gentle Jesus from Sunday school, the man with the Golden Rule, a god of sweet morality that never existed. What do you know of my life in the hot sun, making noon runs for fear of being seen by others?

'Jesus, are you greater than the way of life I have inherited? Are you more than what the church and my parents have told me of you? Are you greater than the urges in me to live life the way I do and seem unable to stop? Honestly, I don't see anything in you that looks like it could be a gift to me. You are just old Jesus, odd and religious with little to say about practical life. I doubt you can pull this off.'

Jesus countered with a description of just what his gift could do for the woman. He gave her knowledge of God which would lead to knowledge of herself. 'Everyone who drinks of this water will be thirsty again, but those who drink of the water I will give them will never be thirsty. The water that I will give will become in them a spring of water gushing up to eternal life.'

He offered the possibility of never being thirsty in the desert sun at noon again. The dailiness of life revolves around perpetual thirst and return to the well again and again without any final satisfaction. Jesus offered an inner source, which could constantly quench a person's thirst with fresh waters. Drawing water, a symbol of routine, could become through Jesus' gift an image of refreshment.

There is a source which can transform daily life from drudgery, and stale water to the gush of living water. Jesus offers living water as a spring that is within us. Its waters well up inside us, gush through us, and give meaning to all of life. The very ordinariness of our days can be enlivened with this splashing, clear, cool water.

Living water brings refreshment. It means continual renewal. Cleansing water flows through, washing us in joy. In living water we have the hope that we do not always need to be cynical and cranky, to be dry and tired. Rather, love and thankfulness can well up through us. This is the possibility of living from the source, of being connected to the wellspring of our lives. The writer of Psalm 87 knew that God is the source of living water when he prayed, 'All my springs are in you.'

What We Give in Exchange

The woman wanted this gift, if only to save her the daily trip. 'Sir, give me this water, so that I may never be thirsty or have to keep coming here to draw water.' Sure, if he could give it to her, she wanted it. It seemed like a nice convenience. Why not have a constant source of water, particularly if it was free? The woman's response considered living water at a literal level. It was a way to make life easier without any work on her part.

We may begin work on a relationship with God at first because we hope it will solve our problems and make us happier. We hope that God will let us live pretty much as we do, with the new twist that we finally enjoy it. I'd like a relationship with God if it means I won't have any dull days, lonely nights, conflicts at work, or financial worries. Yes, since it's free, wave the magic wand; give me the living water.

Of course we don't tap the spring of living water without descending into the depths of our being. God has made us with a spiritual fail-safe mechanism. We receive from God in proportion to our openness before God about ourselves. So, the casual dabbler in a conversation with Jesus will leave disappointed. The knowledge of God that is living water will require a commensurate knowledge of self. And Jesus is not afraid to direct us to that knowledge.

Nor did he hesitate to urge the Samaritan woman deeper. 'Go, call your husband, and come back,' Jesus replied, as if saying, 'So you do want what I have; well then, let's talk, let's deal with your life. I know who you are. Go get your husband.'

She answered him, 'I have no husband.' She wanted to talk about something else. The Samaritan woman tried to seal off that subject with her terse reply.

We may feel as well that there are some areas we would rather not have Jesus bring up. We might say, 'Look, you can be Jesus, and we can talk religion, but don't meddle with closed subjects. I'll clam up if you put your finger on the broken relationships I have been through. You have no right to bring up my parents' expectations and the years I spent trying to please them. I have no need to prove myself anymore.

'Jesus, just drop it. The cheating that I did was years ago; it's a dead subject. I have forgotten it, why don't you leave it alone? I have no more guilt.

'What? Yes, of course I like my work; every job requires sacrifice; every company puts on pressure. How I handle it is not your concern. I have no conflicts with work.'

Life doesn't always turn out the way we hoped. We make the best we can of it; we do the daily routine. And we deny there is a problem. Secretly we want more, but we do not like others to ask about these private yearnings.

Telling Us Who We Are

Jesus, though, was not put off by the woman. 'You are right in saying "I have no husband"; for you have had five husbands, and the one you have now is not your husband. What you have said is true!' Jesus got relentless. He named her life. He said in effect, 'I know you; I know who you are. There is no need to hide.'

How he knew, whether by divine intuition or by her reputation, is not the point. Exactly what she had done or not done to live through five husbands is not the point. The issue was that she was a woman who lived by avoiding the other women, and who lived in guilt and denial. He had a gift for her, but to receive it, she would need to own up to her life.

Similarly, Jesus might reply to our denials, 'You are right in saying you have nothing to prove: you simply feel unworthy all the time. You are right in saying you have no guilt; it has turned to a constant numbness. You are right in saying you have no conflict at work; you gave over your soul and you are sinking.'

Overcoming Resistance

No one likes to admit such brokenness. So the woman used a tactic that has always been popular. She threw up an unanswerable religious question. Her reply tossed it all back on Jesus. 'Sir, I see that you are a prophet. Our ancestors worshipped on this mountain, but you [Jews] say that the place where people must worship is in Jerusalem.' She brought up the old conflict about holy places between Samaritans and Jews. Jesus had become awfully close to breaking down the traditional barriers, so she threw one back up.

When Jesus gets too close to naming us and

making us deal with the complexities of our lives, we may tote out the religious arguments. We sense that God is making a claim on us; Jesus wants to dredge up the truth we keep well hidden. And we may reply, 'Well what about the Buddhists? Will they be saved if they are good people? What about the problem of suffering in the world? How could an all-powerful, all-loving God allow that pain? Isn't religion up to the individual?' We use these standard doubts, which are perfectly legitimate but unanswerable questions, to keep God at bay. Since these contradictions will not be solved any time soon, they make excellent defences against interacting with Jesus.

Of course we cannot minimize the pain within such questions, nor the suffering which leads people to voice them. That very pain, though, can lead us to the depths beneath the cover-ups. The woman's suffering was in part the Samaritan sense of inferiority combined with her own sense of being ostracized. Jesus took her deeper.

'Woman, believe me, the hour is coming when you will worship the Father neither on this mountain nor in Jerusalem. . . . God is spirit, and those who worship him must worship in spirit and truth.' He goes beneath the question of where, to the question of truth. The knowledge of God and the knowledge of self remain intertwined. Spirit and truth require an inner honesty. God desires worship from the heart.

She made one final play at getting away. 'I know that the Messiah is coming... When he comes, he will proclaim all things to us.' This should have been a showstopper. The Messiah was always coming but never came. This was like the 'I-will-get-to-that-when-things-slow-down' gambit.

And Jesus simply took off the gloves. 'I am he, the one who is speaking to you.' He pinned her, communicating: 'There is no escape. The time is now. I am come to reveal your life to you and to reveal God to you. I have living water. There are no more questions except, "What will you do with me?" '

At this point, they were interrupted by the return of the disciples. The woman, though, left her water jar and ran back to the town. She said to everyone, 'Come and see a man who told me everything I have ever done! He cannot be the Messiah, can he?'

As the story concludes, we do not see any great work of healing, or hear of any particular response the woman made. Somehow, though, being known was enough to ignite her life. The woman who drew water in the noonday heat in or-

der to avoid people now ran to tell everyone what
had happened.

To Be Known

There is something marvellous about being
known. Many of us love to take personality tests
and hear about who we are. When someone
describes us, in love, for all our quirks and unique-
ness, we may laugh with involuntary delight. We
long to be discovered. While we may hide much
from others, we nevertheless ache to have them
find out our hiding places.

God desires that we feel known by him,
known fully and still loved. Such intimacy, though,
requires our participation. By acknowledging what
God reveals to us about ourselves, we can cooper-
ate with the Spirit who searches out our depths.
This confession in itself is healing. Vivid energy is
released as suppressed aspects of ourselves are
brought to the light of day.

The Anglican priest Christopher Bryant
writes in his book *Jung and the Christian Way:*

> Directly I change my attitude and admit
> my fault or my folly, not merely verbally
> but with a real inward alteration of feel-
> ing expressed in outward behaviour,

then at once the healing waters begin to flow as from some deep spring within myself; the parched desert begins to blossom and I am inundated with a sense of peace... the renewing grace of God begins to heal and liberate those who turn and submit to this inner law... this life-renewing Spirit flows from the belly, the symbol of a centre within us which is also the seat of powerful emotion.

The belief that God guides us from the centre of our being can completely transform the idea of obedience to God's will.

I remember going on a retreat once with two friends from the church. As the weekend progressed, our talking grew more intimate. I decided to reveal a side of myself of which I have never been pleased, which I keep as well hidden as possible. I said, 'I know that I try to be a nice, caring guy toward you most of the time, but if our friendship continues to deepen, you need to know this about me. I really can be a self-centred, attention-craving, egotistical person.' I said it in all earnestness, with no small degree of fear. My friends started to laugh. 'What's so funny?' I asked. They howled with laughter. 'Do you think you're telling us anything new? We know who you are. We love you just the same.' What I feared to confess for fear of rejection was a characteristic that was completely obvious to my friends. They knew and they still cared. Once I admitted it, though, the release was like living waters.

Jesus offered the woman at the well a spring of living water within her. He offers it to us as well. The price is allowing him to take us into our pasts, into our shadow side, into our brokenness. We discover there that he knows us completely. And he asks that we allow him in those deep, named places to love us in great intimacy. John Calvin knew the healing side of such exploration: 'Accordingly, the knowledge of ourselves not only arouses us to seek God, but also, as it were, leads us by the hand to find him.'

Questions for Reflection

The story of the Samaritan woman is found in John 4:1–42.

1) In what ways may you have felt that Jesus had 'no bucket and the well is deep' in your everyday life?

2) What does 'living water' evoke for you?

3) Complete the sentence: 'If living water were welling up within me, I...'

4) In what areas are you most likely to try and deflect Jesus' inquiries?

5) In what areas of your life would you most like to be known, to be found out and still loved?

6) Imagine that Jesus does know all of you and names those places long hidden. How would you respond?

Exercises

1) Learn the line from the story, 'Sir, give me this water, so that I may never be thirsty.' When you have learned it well enough to say it aloud without referring to your book, take a walk in which you repeat the phrase. Say it with different emphases, in different moods. Try singing it. You can begin by simply lengthening the sounds of the words. Try different tunes as they come to you; do not worry about being musical. Concentrate on expressing the emotion of the phrase.

2) Draw a picture of living water welling up within a person, perhaps yourself. Use the vivid colours of crayons, bright markers, or water colours. A literal rendering is not the goal, but rather an expression of the feeling of living water gushing forth.

3) Reflect upon your drawing. Thinking in terms of yourself, where does the living water get blocked? Where does it flow freely? Where is God, or the source, located?

4) Prayers from different traditions can provide new entrances to Bible stories. Try this prayer from the Russian Orthodox tradition:

> O Saviour, fill my thirsting soul with the waters of godliness, as Thou didst cry to all: If anyone thirst, let him come to me and drink! O Christ God, Fountain of our life, glory to Thee!
>
> The Samaritan Woman came to the well in faith: she saw Thee, the Water of Wisdom, and drank abundantly! She inherited the Kingdom on high and is ever glorified.[1]

Notes

[1]*The Divine Liturgy According to St John Chrysostom,* second edition, St. Tikhon's Seminary Press, South Canaan, PA, 1977, pages 192, 194

~4~

Do You Really Want Something from ME?

IN THE LAST THREE CHAPTERS, WE HAVE CONSIDERED offers which God makes to people. First, in the story of the younger brother, Jesus tells us that God offers to receive us home when we have been far away. Second, the story of the older brother reveals that all the joy that God has is ours if we would simply go into the party. And third, Jesus offered the woman by the well an unending supply of fresh, energizing, living water. In so doing he gave her the gift of knowing her deeply, of naming her innermost self.

God wants us to reconnect. These three offers speak to our deep yearnings for forgiveness, joy, and intimacy. The possibility that even a portion of what Jesus described could be ours is enough to get us moving back towards God.

Now we will look more closely at the other side of his offers. What did Jesus want from the people he encountered? What did it cost them to open up their lives to his way of doing things?

And are we able to stand up to such demands?

Put Out into the Deep

Near the beginning of Jesus' days of teaching and healing, he called twelve people to be his disciples. One morning Jesus was teaching by the Sea of Galilee, and the crowd began to press upon him. He saw two boats tied near the shore, and recognized one of the owners, Simon, who was nearby cleaning his fishing nets. Jesus got into one of the boats and asked Simon to ease out a bit onto the lake. There, the crowds could see him and Jesus could breathe.

When he was finished, he said to Simon, 'Put out into the deep water, and let down your nets for a catch.' Simon answered, 'Master, we have worked all night long but have caught nothing. Yet if you say so, I will let down the nets.'

And when they threw in the nets, they caught so many fish that the nets began to break. Simon called for his partners in the other boat. But even with two boats, there were so many fish that the boats began to sink. Can a fisherman have too many fish?

It was the kind of catch Simon might have dreamed about years ago when as a sleepy boy he tried to stay awake during the long night while his father taught him the trade. But in the next moment Simon didn't care a thing for the fish. The boat was sinking and with it his means of livelihood. Simon, though, was on his knees, with water and fish swirling around him. 'Go away from me, Lord, for I am a sinful man!'

The miracle opened up for him a sense of wonder. In a profound way, Simon realized the power and immediate presence of God. A wondrous sight was followed with a striking awareness of unworthiness. Simon had the sudden gasp of realization, 'If this is God, and this is I, the distance is too great for me to stand. I'm in a lot of trouble!' A panicked moment of horror arose.

We can return to John Calvin for a moment. 'Again it is certain that man never achieves a clear knowledge of himself unless he has first looked upon God's face, and then descends from contemplating him to scrutinize himself.' In this story, Jesus made a request. He asked Simon to put out into the deep water and to let down the nets, only recently cleaned, after a long night of fishing with no catch. Jesus set him up for an experience of the presence of God which would overflow his understanding of the way the world worked. Seeing an act of God, Simon saw himself anew.

I realize the difficulty in discussing experiences of the presence of God. These pages are precisely for people who have trouble connecting with God in the first place, who do not readily apprehend the spiritual realm. Such a sense of wonder as occurred in this story cannot be prescribed. We cannot make it happen.

We can, however, attempt to describe the places and times where it has happened to ordinary people. And if we are bold, we can let down our nets, should we be asked. Our hope will be to try and be aware should God break into our everyday world.

Of course, modern experiences might be much milder, but no less instructive. For example, we may have found ourselves in the presence of something so fine that we felt rough and rude in comparison. The humbling of such a moment was not a debilitating shame but, paradoxically, an uplifting humility. The perception of something wonderfully beyond us may define us as small, but at the same time set us soaring with the taste of beauty.

An adolescent boy goes to meet his date, a girl on the edge of womanhood, and he is overwhelmed with her mystery. He is clumsy and befuddled in the presence of someone so wonderful. Simultaneously the boy feels humbled and exalted. Perhaps without ever being conscious of it, he feels at an intuitive level that her beauty partakes of and points to a higher Beauty.

An aspiring painter discovers something of what it is to capture shades of light, the lines of a face, or the atmosphere of a landscape. One day she stands before Rembrandt's 'The Night Watch', and her very understanding of what it takes to render light and faces leads her to awe. Or should she see Van Gogh's 'Starry Night', this artist might be roused with the painting's passion and, at the same time, humbled by the skill which could create such evocative work. This is more than mere comparison or hero worship. An artist touches upon the Creator's own art.

Once, when I was as far away from Christian faith as I have ever been, I entered the cathedral at Gloucester on a tour. Circumstances were hardly conducive to a religious experience. We had forty-five minutes off the bus. A crowd of tourists was around; the cathedral itself was not spectacular, particularly in comparison to many others. So it was completely by surprise that I was swept away.

I was standing alone in the nave, looking at the vaulted ceiling. The organist had come in to practise, and was playing. The music shifted. One strong, clear bass note sounded. Around that one note the melody swirled. I found that within me, something was bowed to the ground on the steadiness of that note. It called me, brought my soul to its knees, then lifted me up. I did not name the experience *God*; it had no specific content. I just knew what it was to be called, to be brought low and then lifted up; to be a creature in the presence of something high.

More recently, my eight-year-old son grabbed me after church. He said, 'Dad, during the prayer, I felt the presence of God.' I asked him to tell me what it was like. 'I don't know,' he said, 'I've never felt anything like it before; I just felt like God was right there. And it made me cry.' As the firstborn and as a preacher's kid, my son had learned all that he was taught at church and home about God. He had absorbed faithfully and questioned vigorously. On that day, though, suddenly he had something visceral to go with what he knew in his head.

Such religious experiences can come in many forms. One may occur simply while reading; or another immediately following childbirth. We may feel such wonder on top of a mountain, in someone's arms, alone in the woods, or in the middle of a party. The common element is the sense of being in the presence of something far greater than oneself. Suddenly, proper perspective appears, and we realize our finitude. For Simon Peter, the great catch of fish opened his eyes to the power of Jesus. It overwhelmed him. He felt unworthy and unclean. The experience of wonder became painful and frightening. Simon begged Jesus to leave.

Do Not Be Afraid

Jesus spoke right through Simon's fear. 'Do not be afraid; from now on you will be catching people.' The effect of those words was to say, 'I know who you are and I have something for you to do; do not fear what you are not—I will make you into something more.' The miracle brought Simon to his knees; Jesus lifted him up with a word of assurance and an assignment.

Casting nets for fish was finished. Could he have fished again after this great haul anyway? His life's work had been filled up to such a point that any future pursuit of it became trivial. Now Jesus asked Simon to help him fish for people. He wanted help from Simon and the others.

Jesus wanted to help Simon see beyond the boundaries of daily experience. Jesus was calling back the world to the love of God. He invited the disciples into that love, but not just so they could bask there. Jesus wanted some help, some workers for his mission.

To secure his participation, Jesus showed Simon a miracle that opened him to the reality beyond ordinary reality. Simon saw vividly that God exists and interacts with the world. Such knowledge was enough to overwhelm him, even to ruin him if he had been left alone. But Jesus went on to address the terrible vacuum: 'Do not be afraid,' and to issue the call, 'From now on you will be fishing for people.'

In a similar passage in the book of Isaiah (chapter 6), the prophet had a vision of the throne of God, and he cried out in dismay, 'Woe is me! I am lost, for I am a man of unclean lips.' In the next moment, one of the heavenly creatures around the throne touched his lips with a fiery coal and declared, 'Now that this has touched your lips, your guilt has departed and your sin is blotted out.' Then, Isaiah heard the voice of the Lord saying, 'Whom shall I send, and who will go for us?' Isaiah replied, 'Here am I; send me!'

This process moved Isaiah, as it did Simon, through awe to unworthiness. Then each was taken from a declaration of forgiveness to a request for service. The response to such a dramatic calling was one of complete commitment.

The very same drama may be played out today. For many people, there is a season of transformation in their lives. It may not be recognized until years later, but then the pattern emerges. There was a growing apprehension of God's reality in conjunction with a personal crisis. When the storm passed, there occurred a renewed commitment and deeper connection to God. Perhaps we can outline this process in an example.

Suppose you have been plying your trade upon the seas. You've been living your life, working out things the best you can. You haven't been particularly interested in religion. It was part of your life as a child, but hasn't meant much recently. God may seem the right thing for sweet innocents, but none of them would understand the things you have thought and done. The idea of active faith seems too legalistic, too concerned with petty righteousness. You can't imagine yourself being a Bible-toting, hymn-singing, evangelistic holy person. That would never do. You'd just as soon leave God alone if God will leave you alone.

But the years pass and more questions eat at you now; maybe it's just because you don't sleep like you used to. Sometimes you feel as if you've been fishing all night, and have caught nothing.

You've dropped your nets, hauled them in over and over again, and there's nothing to show for it but a cranky mood and a tired body.

But then there's a subtle suggestion in your mind. Why don't you go ahead and go to church a couple of times? At least the family will be pleased; it won't hurt anything. Or why don't you go ahead and see the counsellor—let some of those feelings out—it can't hurt. Why not just talk with your spouse about how you're feeling; there's so much water under the bridge now, there's nothing to lose. It's all very benign at first. A tiny growl of spiritual hunger nudges you just a little way.

And it works out fine. It feels good to be at church. Talking an hour a week with that counsellor eases the stress. And your spouse appreciates the conversation. This is a better way to live.

But then there's another suggestion. A little more outrageous. 'Put out into the deep water and let down your nets for a catch.' Think about the life that you live and know so well from a different point of view. What if it wasn't just about what you want and need, but about what God wants from you? What if you unfolded your nets, just let them down and took a look at what you've been living for all these years? Can you be bold enough to ask what you've been longing for? Just unravel your nets in the deep and see what happens.

For many people, there is quite suddenly a great haul of fish in the nets. It may be in church, in the counsellor's office, over dinner with your spouse, or in the middle of a fight. But quite dramatically it dawns upon you: There is a God. There's more to life than what you have been seeing. There is a God. And God makes a claim on your life.

Perhaps at the very same moment, you get a whole different view of yourself. Scales fall off. It is horrible. 'I've been living for me. I've been curved in on myself all these years, and it makes me sick. All the love lost! All the betrayals—by neglect as much as anything! The blindness! Woe is me. I'm a mess that can't be fixed. I've got to close all these thoughts up and get out of here.' The boat is sinking.

But then, if you are blessed, just as soon as the horror of self-knowledge is embraced, there comes another feeling of presence. A gentle voice which speaks from the depths of the soul, even from the depths of the universe. 'It's all right. Do not be afraid. I know who you are. Forgiveness is mine to grant. I'm not here to destroy your life. I'm here to remake it.' It feels like death at first, but then there is new life. 'See, this coal upon your lips makes them clean. I remove your sins.'

The sudden apprehension of God's reality

creates a sudden knowledge of self. And you perceive a horrible gap between yourself and God. But immediately into the breach God pours love and forgiveness. There is an intuition that God knows full well who you are and loves you anyway. Beneath the crisis of the meaning of life, whatever form it takes, God gives a sense that all is well and you are kept in love. God lifts you out of the sinking boat.

But there is always one more act in the play. The sense of God's claim comes again, not to undo you with unworthiness, but to rouse you to a higher calling. In contemporary language, your response may be, 'OK, I'm yours. I'll live as your child; I want what you want more than anything. I need your love that much. I will serve you.'

The New Occupation

Such a commitment may occur gradually over time, or in a burst of devotion. Either way, from the time we become consciously aware of Jesus' calling, ordinary life ceases more and more to occupy centre stage. We live for something deeper and higher. The work we do, we know now, could be burst through with such a fulfilment that it would make us quake. All that we strive for, which we used to think was so important to our happiness, could be fulfilled in a moment and we would count it worth nothing in the face of God.

This new activity of fishing for people may or may not be externally different from our current daily work. The key change is in the perspective from which we view people and tasks. We live now with a new sense of purpose in life: we are to be channels of God's love. We have a mission.

This may seem frightening if we have barely begun to realize how much God loves us. It may seem impossible that we should be calling other people to the love of God when we have just arrived home, just stepped into the party, just had a first sip of living water.

But there is a principle of flow in the life that is connected to God. Jesus never intended his healing love to sit stagnant inside us. Living water bubbles and gushes as it passes into us, through us, and out of us.

I am aware that following this story all the way to its dramatic conclusion may have leapfrogged us beyond where you are at the present time. Such commitment may be too much at this stage. We will look at several other approaches. In the next chapters, we will look more at what Jesus asked of people and the way in to his love and to a sense of purpose in our living.

Questions for Reflection

The story of the great catch of fish is found in Luke 5:1–11.

1) For what do you cast your nets daily? When have you felt like you've been out all night and caught nothing?

2) Using the imagery of the story, in what waters might God be calling you to let down your nets into the deep? That is to say, in what areas of your life do you feel God might be nudging you towards a greater openness for transformation?

3) How might God desire to reorient the work of your life?

4) Simon was struck with a sense of his unworthiness in the face of the miracle. Are there ways in which you feel unworthy of God's love and attention? What reassurance would help you?

5) Can you remember an experience of awe, the feeling of being in the presence of something or someone very much greater than yourself, which gave a feeling of humility?

6) Today, getting more than we could imagine of what we work for might simply make us feel worthy and inflated. How might God so overflow the strivings of daily life to open your eyes to the deeper purposes in living?

7) How can we today be fishers of people? How might such a vocation be worked out in your life?

8) What would it mean to you to be able to do something for Jesus, to carry out a work for him?

Exercises

1) Using crayons or markers, draw a picture of your nets overflowing with what you strive for in your life. When you have completed your drawing, consider if this abundance is enough to satisfy you. Consider if the God who overflows the nets could give an invitation so compelling that you would leave the catch on the shore. Repeating the words, 'Follow me and I will make you fishers of people,' lay aside your drawing and imagine going to follow Jesus.

2) Dag Hammarskjöld has written in his autobiography, *Markings*, of a time when his life was reoriented to a higher purpose:

> I don't know who—or what—put the question, I don't know when it was put. I don't even remember answering. But at some moment I did answer *Yes* to Someone—or Something—and from that hour I was certain that existence is meaningful and that, therefore, my life in self-surrender, had a goal.
>
> From that moment I have known what it means 'not to look back', and 'to take no thought for the morrow'.

Compare his experience to that of Simon in our story. Write down any experiences you can recall of answering 'Yes' to Someone beyond you.

3) Read this poem by George Herbert as a prayer:

Love [III]

Love bade me welcome: yet my soul drew back,
  Guilty of dust and sin.
But quick-eyed Love, observing me grow slack
  From my first entrance in,
Drew nearer to me, sweetly questioning,
  If I lacked anything.

'A guest', I answered, 'worthy to be here.'
  Love said, 'You shall be he.'
'I, the unkind, ungrateful? Ah my dear,
  I cannot look on thee.'
Love took my hand, and smiling did reply,
  'Who made the eyes but I?'

'Truth, Lord, but I have marred them: let my
 shame
  Go where it doth deserve.'
'And know you not', says Love, 'who bore the
 blame?'
  'My dear, then I will serve.'
'You must sit down', says Love, 'and taste my
 meat.'
  So I did sit and eat.

~5~

How Can I Do This?

UNFORTUNATELY, FEW OF US HAVE AN EXPERIENCE like Simon's great catch of fish. We do not get overwhelmed with God's presence and see our lives changed immediately. I am aware that even the use of such language may provoke resistance in those searching tentatively for a deeper relationship with God through Jesus.

Resistance to the call of God is inevitable. Even though we yearn for God, we still baulk at the terms offered. Far too often we sit thirsty by the well or lonely outside the party. And it is the issue of resistance that our next story addresses.

Once Jesus was setting out on a journey when a man ran up to him, fell on his knees before Jesus, and asked, 'Good Teacher, what must I do to inherit eternal life?' Immediately, we see that this encounter is going to be straightforward; the man wants to know, 'How do I connect?' The phrase 'to inherit eternal life' meant not only life everlasting which goes beyond existence in the present world; it meant living life today in fulfilling accord with

God's will.[1] This is a loaded phrase, full of the meanings we have been after. Eternal life is the life of living water, ever fresh. The man was asking, 'How do I live an abundant, lively life?'

Immediately, Jesus slowed the man down. He deflected the man's opening flattery. 'Why do you call me good? No one is good but God alone.' Again, it is helpful to think of the phrases from that time. Strict Jews reserved the title of good for God. But the Greek culture of the time might use such a phrase liberally for esteemed teachers. Using this phrase, the man showed high reverence for Jesus in a culturally sophisticated manner. Jesus, however, took the opportunity to turn the attention from himself to God.

Jesus went on to answer the man's question with a standard instruction in piety. The way to a life of blessing was, as everyone knew, through keeping the Law. 'You know the commandments: "You shall not murder; You shall not commit adultery; You shall not steal; You shall not bear false witness; You shall not defraud; Honour your father and mother."' This is an interesting list. All but defrauding are taken from the Ten Commandments. And they are the easier, more obvious of the commandments for a decent person to keep.

This list is much like the popular conception of being a Christian. 'Oh, you know, Do unto others and try to be a good person.' On a surface level, these commandments are not much for meeting the hunger in our souls. Keeping our noses clean is fine but does not connect us to God.

What an insightful teacher Jesus was. He threw out a stereotypical answer to see on what level the man was seeking. If he had been a superficial seeker, simply wanting a stamp of approval for the way he was living, Jesus' answer would have been enough. He could have gone away, left in his shallowness. But a person with a restless soul could not easily take that list and leave it.

'Teacher, I have kept all these since my youth.' The implication is that he was not satisfied. The young man had lived a good life; he had been a good guy, one who did the right thing, and he needed more. This man was not the younger brother type who went off and squandered his inheritance; he was more like the older brother who stayed home and did what was required of him. Today, he would be someone who has been in the church, no stranger to the language of faith. We could meet him in the pews.

This is the man who works hard during the week, comes to church on Sunday, sits respectfully, and has the admiration of his peers. He ushers two months a year, serves on a finance committee, and generally contributes his share of time and money.

Most of the time everything is fine, but once in a while comes the nagging doubt, 'Is this all there is? Am I doing the right thing? Shouldn't I be feeling more?' As youth turns to middle age, the question of meaning arises. He wants to know more about what he needs to do.

This is the woman who has helped out on all the standard committees. She has taught at Bible holiday clubs. Every week she has dressed the children and taken them to church in the typical Sunday morning mad dash. A hundred covered dishes have been received from her hands. When the prayer chain called, she prayed. Once a year the women's group met at her house. All these things she has done since her youth. And still there is some lack. What else should she do?

One Thing You Lack

When the man had implied his dissatisfaction with standard religious observance, Jesus evidently was moved. Mark records this wonderful line, 'Jesus, looking at him, loved him.' Of course Jesus loved everyone he met. But articulating his love at this moment meant that something in particular had moved Jesus. The man's honest searching evoked love in Jesus. And this feeling of affection surrounds what Jesus was about to say.

He spoke to this man in love, with hopes of meeting his need.

'You lack one thing; go, sell what you own, and give the money to the poor, and you will have treasure in heaven; then come, follow me.' For the man who had everything, one thing was missing: giving away what he had. What he lacked was not doing something more or obtaining something else; he needed to clear out some of what he had.

It is important to realize here that Jesus' advice, as wild as it sounds to our ears, was even more astonishing in the culture of first century Judaism. People felt that riches were a sign of God's favour. Having a lot meant blessings had been given in reward for righteous living. Of course, giving a tithe had been part of the culture; as well as the understanding that one should be openhanded to the poor. But giving up everything would have been tossing God's blessings back, a sign of disrespect. The man would have been making himself like the unrighteous and the unblessed; all signs of spiritual achievement would have been relinquished.

Jesus, looking at him, loved him, then asked him in love to strip himself of all signs of God's favour. He was to start again.

Emptying out, not achieving more, was the way to inherit eternal life. Leaving it all would clear the way to follow Jesus. It is interesting that this story follows immediately upon the story of the blessing of the children.

The Way of a Child

People had been bringing their small children to Jesus in order that he might touch them and give them a blessing. The disciples didn't like all this crowding and tried to send the people away. But Jesus stopped them. He said, 'Truly I tell you, whoever does not receive the kingdom of God as a little child will never enter it.' Once again, this story predates our culture. Judaism had not passed through a cycle of the adoration of children and the elevation of their needs; no cultural esteem for the innocence of childhood had made Jesus' words sentimental or even welcome. Children were economically and socially unimportant. They could not achieve or produce. Children must simply receive what is given. So, the kingdom of God, this life of connectedness to all God has for us, is evidently a gift for those without sufficient claim to it. And, in fact, all claims of worthiness become a hindrance. The kingdom is a gift.

This story appears to be in contrast to the story of the older brother we considered in Chapter Two. The father in that parable said, 'Son, you are always with me, and all that I have is yours.'

In this story of the rich man, Jesus said, 'Sell what you own, and give the money to the poor… then come, follow me.' On the one hand, all things are ours. Whatever we have been seeking is already within reach. All that God has, which is everything, has been given to us. But on the other hand nothing is ours. Which is true? Are we those who can joyfully lay claim to all of God? Or are we those who must live in poverty for Jesus' sake?

It seems to be a matter of possession. And again the image of children is helpful. The child may partake of all the parents have. Every blessing and possession, every privilege may be bestowed before any merit can lay claim to earning such abundance.

The child may enjoy the parents' resources, but the child does not have legal entitlement; may not buy or sell at will, may not supplant the parents.

When we are stripped of claims of achievement and worthiness, then we are open to receiving all. If we think we have leverage on God to demand blessing, then we are blocked from it. If we feel we have enough on our own to satisfy us; if we hold to what we have as our own, then God will ask for it.

The heart of this passage is that Jesus does ask us for something. He asks for ultimate allegiance. He wants God to be at the centre of our being. Control is released into the hands of God; will is surrendered. My way must give way to God. In 'Little Gidding', T. S. Eliot has written of 'A condition of complete simplicity/(Costing not less than everything.)' And in 'East Coker' he explains,

> In order to possess what you do not possess
>   You must go by the way of dispossession.
> In order to arrive at what you are not
>   You must go through the way in which you
>   are not.
> And what you do not know is the only thing
>   you know
> And what you own is what you do not own
> And where you are is where you are not.

We have uncovered the great paradox of Christian faith. God desires to give us everything. God demands that we give up everything for him. When we hold on to what we have in defiance of what God requires, we are disconnected and cut off from the way of life. When we are stripped of all achievement, when the hand opens and lets control slip away, then, and only then, does God respond with the gift of all things. We are blocked so often from a life of connection and joy, not because God will not give, but because we will not release.

Of course no one wants to do this. It is contra-rational to let go of what we have in hopes of what an invisible God may give.

The man in the story, who came with such high hopes, could not immediately accept Jesus' words. Mark tells us, 'When he heard this, he was shocked and went away grieving, for he had many possessions.' Precisely what he possessed blocked him. The man was sad. Was he grieved because he knew that his whole life had been spent acquiring and managing his position and wealth? Was he sad because he would soon be giving up all he had worked for? Was it astonishment that all these years he had worked so hard for the wrong thing? We do not know if later he took Jesus' advice or not.

We can imagine the difficulty.

We may find that we are so enmeshed in our way of life that change seems nearly impossible. Though we long for a connection to God, old loyalties keep a grip upon us. It goes against our grain to have to count our achievements as worthless.

We cannot say exactly what Jesus asks of each

person. It may very well be a literal giving up of whatever we prize more than God. This is stunning, particularly if we know little of God and have little reason to trust that a relationship with God will fulfil us. Jesus went right for the heart. He did it in love, but he was no less demanding for his compassion. He wants it all.

It is enough to make you put these pages down and go away disappointed. You had hoped, perhaps, for so much more. And this is intolerable. The disciples too were amazed. 'Then who can be saved?' they said to one another. Jesus looked at them and said, 'For mortals it is impossible, but not for God; for God all things are possible.'

No one is so enmeshed that there are no cracks in the armour. If you are still interested, there is a way in, and we shall consider it in the next chapter.

Questions for Reflection

The story of the rich man is found in Mark 10:17–27.

1) In what ways have you tried to live your life as a 'good' person in the conventional sense? How has that been satisfying? What, if anything, is lacking?

2) The rich man asked about eternal life. If you could ask Jesus one question pertinent to the living of your life, what would it be?

3) Jesus asked the rich man to sell all he had and give it to the poor. What kinds of possessions, responsibilities, habits or activities block your following of Jesus?

4) What do you fear Jesus will ask of you? What do you hope he will ask of you? From what demands would you turn away sad?

Exercises

1) Do you think the man sold everything?
Write a paragraph which tells what he did in the next couple of days; perhaps write one from each perspective. Then, write a paragraph in which Jesus says to you, 'One thing you lack . . .' Explore what he asks of you and how you respond.

2) Try praying this prayer, *A Covenant Prayer in the Wesleyan Tradition*.

I am no longer my own, but thine.
Put me to what thou wilt, rank me with whom
   thou wilt.
Put me to doing, put me to suffering.
Let me be employed by thee or laid aside for
   thee,
exalted for thee or brought low by thee.
Let me be full, let me be empty.
Let me have all things, let me have nothing.
I freely and heartily yield all things
   to thy pleasure and disposal.
And now, glorious and blessed God,
Father, Son, and Holy Spirit,
thou art mine, and I am thine. So be it.
And the covenant which I have made on earth,
let it be ratified in heaven.

Notes

1 William Lane's excellent commentary on Mark's Gospel has provided the historical background for this chapter. William Lane, *The Gospel of Mark*, William B. Eerdmans, Grand Rapids, 1974, pages 363–370

~6~

In through the Back Door

I REMEMBER THE SPRING AFTERNOON SEVERAL YEARS ago which was the turning point in some personal counselling I was undertaking. The therapist and I had talked for many weeks about my life and relationships. Being a dutiful patient, I had admitted freely many instances of selfishness and betrayal of which I was neither proud, nor, to be honest, particularly ashamed. There was, of course, something else we were trying to uncover.

As we moved closer to it, whatever it was, I remember feeling more and more like a little boy. I grew increasingly embarrassed. Today I do not even recall what it was I had to declare. I only know it was some admission of bald need, of wilting selfishness, of some little thing I had done which had no gloss of charm or style to it. It had no grandiosity of 'big sin.' It was just there. A raw little nugget of my essential neediness.

When I finally spoke it into the open air, I thought, 'Now that will do it. She will realize how petty and childish I am. She will know that I have no big problem; she will discontinue the therapy. I don't deserve to be here anyway.'

But my counsellor did not flinch. Her expression stayed exactly the same as it had been. She listened and accepted. Of course she knew what I was revealing. I think she could tell that I was ready to be sprawled on the pin. But there was no accusation. She simply received it as another part of me. We went on, and I was free.

I danced out of the office and laughed a belly laugh all the way home. People in the staid streets of that town stared at me, but I didn't care. I was free. Someone had seen inside me, to the pettiest, to the worst, and still accepted me. My healing had begun. I was learning how to love—because I had been loved in that specific way.

In the last chapter, we saw that Jesus asked for 'not less than everything' from the man who had approached him. Such a demand seemed almost impossible to meet; perhaps you felt your own resistance to giving yourself away arise. This head-on approach raises our defiance. Approaching God from a position of strength did not get the rich man very far; you can't get in that way.

In another story, Jesus took a different tack. The one who came to him led with her need, not her strength. Her story resolved not in sad walking away, but in peace and forgiveness. Perhaps this is a way in for us as well.

Drawn to Find Jesus

In the seventh chapter of Luke, we read of a woman who heard that Jesus was in town and went to find him. She had a reputation in her village of being a 'sinner'. Luke does not tell us exactly what she had done, but the label seems indelible. I wonder what in Jesus drew her to him. Word may have reached the common people that Jesus was not intimidated by the rich or the righteous. He did not mind being seen with misfits. Jesus dared to put his hands on the sick. The forgotten were noticed by him. He looked at them; he spoke to them; he touched them.

As she made her way through the streets, she may have tried to recall how long it had been since anyone had touched her with tenderness. How long had it been since anyone had looked at her without first seeing the label of her sin blazoned across her face?

Everyone in that tiny town knew who she was; there was never an escape. She had no place to go; if only someone would come for her. It had been months since anyone had even spoken kindly.

'Was there ever a time', she wondered, 'when I did not have the weight of these memories around my neck? Did I ever walk lightly through the streets? I am reminded always, every time I see someone, of who I am: a sinner. Joseph is a carpenter; Ruth is a seamstress; Ben is a priest; and I am a sinner. To them I do no good. I have no occupation. I do not breathe or have needs or wonder about the weather like other people. I am simply a sinner. Touch me and touch sin. Speak to me and your tongue is filthy. Look at me and see the discarded.'

So she went to find Jesus; he was going to dinner at the house of Simon, a Pharisee. Such events were normally open to acceptable visitors. She would risk going; she could not help it. 'What could a Pharisee do to me now anyway? Let him scowl; he does that all the time as it is. If only Jesus would let me near him; if only he might once look at me and see me for something other than my label, see the me behind my shame. One look; one touch; one word; I would give anything.'

She brought with her an alabaster flask, filled with perfume. It was one of the costliest gifts one could give. For the flask itself had to be broken in order to use the perfumed ointment. It was a one-time, perishable gift, solely for the immediate comfort of the recipient. A gift of love.

The woman entered the house, passing the other guests, ignoring their whispers. She made her way to the table, and no one dared to stop her. At last she found that she was standing behind Jesus. She had never seen him before; she knew him as the only stranger and by something else she could not name. He did not turn around. But she began to cry.

She wept for the weight of it all. For all the reasons she should not be there, for all that she regretted. Oh the wretched ash heap of her life! And she cried that she could do nothing else but go there. As usual, her life was out of control. She was ever swept along by forces she didn't understand. And she wept all the more as she realized she was standing within a foot of Jesus. He had seen her now, and she was still there. He had not rejected her out of hand.

'I wish I could touch him, just the least part of him—just his feet.' And she saw that her tears were falling onto his feet, which were stretched out as he leaned on his side at the table. Then all her care in the world was for those feet. Her whole life, all her feelings and pent-up love fell in tears upon his tired, dirty feet. She pulled the clasp and let down her hair, defying the immodesty of it. She wiped his feet with her hair.

'Could I but soothe you for a moment?' she thought. 'Will you have this comfort I can give? Do not turn from me now. Find ease from your travels; I can make your feet feel better. Oh, take my love. It is all I have, and it is yours.' She kissed his feet and poured the perfume on them. She could see that its sweet smell did seem to soothe his tiredness. Her gentle touch accepted Jesus with love and adoration.

The Scandal of Forgiveness

For a moment Jesus found ease in her gift. He closed his eyes to receive this brief comfort from the weight of his ministry. He did not reject her; he did not tell her to stop. Jesus did not turn away though she revealed the most embarrassing vulnerability here in public.

When Jesus opened his eyes, Simon the Pharisee was glowering at him. Simon was furious. His thoughts raced. 'How could he accept the ministrations of a woman such as this, and in my house, and in front of half the town? She has made a spectacle and he doesn't care. Why, it's obscene! If he were really a prophet of God, he would know what kind of woman this is who is touching him— a sinner.'

Jesus knew who she was; and he knew that Simon was full of gall. Jesus told him a story and asked him a question. 'A certain creditor had two debtors; one owed five hundred denarii, and the other fifty. When they could not pay, he cancelled the debts for both of them. Now which of them will love him more?'

Simon was insulted by such an obvious question. But he still bit the hook and answered, 'I suppose the one for whom he cancelled the greater debt.'

Jesus then said with words so simple they must have burned Simon, 'You have judged rightly... Do you see this woman? I entered your house; you gave me no water for my feet, but she has bathed my feet with her tears and dried them with her hair. You gave me no kiss, but from the time I came in she has not stopped kissing my feet. You did not anoint my head with oil, but she has anointed my feet with ointment. Therefore, I tell you, her sins, which were many, have been forgiven; hence she has shown great love. But the one to whom little is forgiven, loves little.'

The woman could hardly believe what she was hearing. As she watched, Jesus turned to her again and said to her, 'Your sins are forgiven.' He told her she was free. She was herself once more, not her label, not her past, not her shame.

'I'm me again,' she thought. 'I'm clean. The master said so. I am not a sinner any more. I am a woman, who sins, yes, but who is forgiven. My life is not my sin any more; my life is my love, and he is everything to me!'

Then, after all the guests had gasped and murmured that Jesus should dare to pronounce forgiveness, and especially for one such as she, he spoke to her again. 'Your faith has saved you. Go in peace.'

Uncovering the Wounds That Lead Us to God

There is no magic formula for connecting with God. The story of this woman tells us that there is only unique, personal, messy encounter. The possibility that if we go to him, he will accept us, nudges our souls toward Jesus. Like the woman of the village, we would be drawn to him if we heard he was in town.

The wounds which lead us to find Jesus are many and varied. We might cry for all the ways we have not been loved in the past. Too many expectations, too much shame; too little attention, too much figuring it out on our own. We do not feel worth very much, and our tears are made of anger as much as sorrow. And sometimes we are stricken to think of what we have done in the name of love to get what we needed that had been withheld. Or worse, the ways we paid back those who did not meet our needs. If you came and stood behind Jesus, finding that your presence was silently accepted, over what would you weep?

To grasp that what has been done cannot be undone might cause tears to come spilling out of us in despair. The dead cannot be called back for reconciliation now; the marriage is over; the children have moved away: and there is nothing we can do about it any more.

Some of us have given away too much of ourselves, given to another person the devotion meant only for God. And we have seen that lesser hands have not held our hearts kindly.

Some have poured love down the pit of another's addiction; all our intuition said it was the right thing to do. But in that black hole, all the rules are reversed. Suddenly we discover that we did not help, but contributed to the addiction. Our sacrifice was in vain, and we mourn.

Some of us have seized control over others. We have wanted to mould people into our image. We have wanted to be God and attempted to crush those who would not take the bait of that idolatry. Every moment is managed by us. And we are so tired from it.

Some will cry that they have tried to please for so long that they have become master manipulators. They have received attention and power, but cannot trust it, for they always angled for it. They feel they must for ever keep on earning acceptance. To let down the guard would be to free fall over the abyss of rejection.

The Healing Acceptance

Of course, in this process, Simon the Pharisee continually urges us to quit; to leave his presence; to go back home and behave. He hisses that we should keep our place; not bother God. We need not try to change, for people such as we can never change.

Simon, however, does not have the final word. Nor does our fear or even our pain. Jesus receives the tears and does not reject us. He speaks the word of forgiveness; he pronounces peace and sets us on the way to wholeness.

The stages of this process are crucial. The first move is his. Jesus comes to town. Somehow in the midst of our daily living, we hear that one such as Jesus exists and can be encountered. Hope arises that life can be different. That is God's work.

The next move is ours. In the second phase, we are open to going to him, knowing that being in his presence will set our wounds oozing and our tears flowing. In that embarrassing pain, the critical step of faith is to turn our shame into an act of love.

Gratitude arises as he receives us. We want to do something in return. We want to show him love.

Jesus, of course, helps us. The third stage occurs concurrently with our confession. The more we reveal, the more we discover that we are not rejected. The more we are accepted, the more likely it is that we will be moved to love and devotion. He is faithful to meet us almost immediately with a sense of forgiveness if we will be honest and open in his presence. He declares, 'Your sins are forgiven; go in peace.'

The fourth stage is typical as well. A voice of doubt arises.

Simon appears, in the guise of those people who work against us or as a voice within our minds. He reasserts our unworthiness and tries to make our situation seem hopeless. Simon can only be answered by the love of Jesus. We do not have the resources alone to combat him.

The final movement in this dance of transformation belongs to us. We accept the word of forgiveness and go our way no longer bound to the habits, the labels, and the destructive behaviour which previously undid us. We are those to whom a word of Jesus has been spoken. We live for him.

There is a similarity between this story and the one about Simon the disciple and the great catch of fish. Both characters moved through confession to forgiveness to a changed life. The active love of Jesus made the difference in turning despair into joy. By contrast, the rich man in the previous story did not move into any position of confession or weakness. We did not see him coming undone within the time frame of the account. He did not, at least immediately, give up his power or position. And so he went away sad. The way in to the kingdom of God seems to be by dropping strength and following weakness.

Will It Work?

I cannot prove to you that Jesus will accept you, should you come into his presence to let down your guard. I can tell you that the whole character of Jesus as we meet him in the Gospels suggests this kind of love. 'Come to me, all you that are weary, and are carrying heavy burdens, and I will give you rest,' said Jesus in a famous passage (Matthew 11:28). I can tell you as well that this love has been true for me and others, as it was for the woman in the story. In Jesus' presence we may safely drop our strengths and reveal our weakness.

You may need to do this kind of confession in the presence of another person, to help you through the crisis of getting it out. Some will work through therapy, some with a spiritual counsellor, some with a friend or in a group. Some will just need to be quietly in the presence of God, on their knees or in the shower, on a walk or in a sanctuary.

Such admission of sin and shame is the way to health. The popular wisdom is backwards when it denounces Christianity's emphasis on owning fault and admitting unworthiness. This kind of confession does not produce a negative self-concept. The bad self-image comes when we try to justify ourselves, when we confess on the surface without opening our souls. When we try to be worthy, we feel for ever unworthy. But when we finally break down the walls and let our profound sense of unworthiness flow, God provides the grace which puts us together from the inside out.

My counsellor brought me to forgiveness by accepting the worst I had to offer. The woman in our story was made whole because Jesus accepted her love. He did not flinch at her presence. He did not recoil from her touch. Nor did he turn from her tears. He received her gift of love as she poured out her life. And by that accepting love she was healed.

Which came first, her faith or his love? It does not matter. It took faith to go to a Pharisee's house in search of love. It takes faith, in the presence of all the voices that condemn us, to open up the old wounds before God. Jesus' love drew her there.

His love draws us now. One elicits the other: faith and forgiving love. They circle around each other in glorious harmony.

I wish you the courage to enter that loop and be swept up in the healing love of Jesus.

Questions for Reflection

The story of the woman who anointed Jesus' feet is found in Luke 7:36–50.

1) What about Jesus in this story draws you to him?

2) We learned from this story that we are led into a deeper connection with God not by our strengths but by our weakness. Using that criterion, what areas in your life might lead you down the path to greater intimacy with God?

3) If you came and stood behind Jesus, over what would you weep?

4) What might inspire your love for him?

5) What part of you, like Simon the Pharisee, would be offended or embarrassed by your crying and your anointing of Jesus' feet? In other words, what blocks your experience of forgiveness and

the accompanying wholeness?

6) What could Jesus say that would effectively answer your Simon?

7) Jesus said to the woman, 'Your faith has saved you; go in peace.' If we had only this story to use, how would you define faith? Use as many concrete verbs and nouns as you can, in preference to abstract ideas.

Exercises

1) The woman's alabaster flask was an extravagant gift of great worth, a gift of love, to be used all at once. What might be your alabaster flask? In other words, what would you like to give Jesus as a gift of love? Try to find, make, write, or draw some token which represents this gift.

2) Mime the woman's (and your) encounter with Jesus, the weeping and the giving of the gift. When you are finished, say aloud the words of Jesus, 'I tell you, her sins, which are many, have been forgiven; hence she has shown great love.'

3) Read and meditate on the words of the song, 'The Feet of Christ', written as a meditation on this story by my dear friend, Ric Smith.

The Feet of Christ

Tired feet, covered with the dirt of the day,
    Neglected, unwashed by the host.
Tears wash you cleaner and hair dries you better
    than basin and towel.
O feet, I weep and worship you.

Strong feet, broken by the miles on the move,
    With walking and standing so long.
Perfume is fragrant, but merit richer
    Than my best anointing.
O feet, I weep and worship you.

Christ's feet, bloodied by the spikes of your Cross;
    Your motion is stilled for a time.
Wood is too cruel a frame for your beauty,
    Your pain is my heartbreak.
O feet, I weep and worship you.[1]

4) Read this prayer from St John Chrysostom, as a way of identifying with the woman in the story.

O Lord, I know that I am not worthy nor sufficiently pleasing that Thou shouldst come under the roof of the house of my soul for it is entirely desolate and fallen in ruin and Thou wilt not find in me a place worthy to lay Thy head. But as Thou didst humble Thyself from on high for our sake, so now humble Thyself to my lowliness. . . .

And as Thou didst not cast out the prostitute, the sinful woman who came to touch Thee, so have compassion on me a sinner who comes to touch Thee.

And as Thou didst not abhor the kiss of her sin-stained and unclean mouth, do not abhor my mouth, worse stained and more unclean than hers, nor my stained and shamed and unclean lips, nor still more my impure tongue.

But let the fiery coal of Thy most pure Body and Thy most precious Blood bring me sanctification, enlightenment and strengthening of my lowly soul and body, relief from the burden of my many transgressions.[2]

5) Write your own prayer to Jesus, expressing the flow of this story as it relates to your life. Pray something of why you are drawn to Jesus, something of what you would weep over, something of what Jesus would say in response to your tears, and something of the ways you would like to be devoted to him.

Notes

[1] Richard A. Smith, 'The Feet of Christ', copyright © 1990, unpublished, used by permission

[2] *The Divine Liturgy According to St John Chrysostom*, second edition, St Tikhon's University Press, South Canaan, PA, 1967, pages 93–94

~7~

Taking a Towel and a Basin

THE ACCOUNT OF THE WOMAN WHO ANOINTED Jesus' feet led us to see that we connect most deeply with God when we lead with our weakness. Coming into God's presence with openness and an honest reading of our lives seems to elicit a response of forgiving grace.

I am hopeful that after reading the stories of the calling of the disciples, the question of the rich man, and the restoration of the woman who anointed Jesus' feet, you will have felt the urge to offer your life into God's care. Those who have had such seasons of surrender to God consistently report a great change for the better in their lives.

No one moment, of course, is ever enough. The life of spiritual deepening is one of process. We spiral in and out of being open to our desire to be in God's presence. Some days we are highly resistant. Other times it seems that long locked doors open with the easiest touch and we are ushered straight into an audience with God. The very next day, we may simply not have the energy nor even feel the need to do this difficult inner work.

I cannot know how far along you are in your inner openness to God. I would like now, however, to move to the way in which such openness finds concrete expression in daily life. For those who are still considering putting out into the deep, selling their treasures, or anointing the feet of Jesus, these next stories will be a preview of what Jesus asks from us if we go further with him.

The inner life requires, after the initial stages, a corresponding expression in the outer life. This is by no means automatic. Like everything else, outer change requires conscious intention. A blossoming inner life can be the source for such change, but ultimately we have to will ourselves to move ahead. Our connection with God provides the motivation and energy to enact our intentions.

In other words, we are considering the question, 'If you were to follow your longing to go home, if you were to receive living water, if you were to follow Jesus, what would that look like, not just in terms of inner personal growth, but in the concrete world?'

A Service to Be Passed Along

The Gospel of John records an event which took place the evening of the Last Supper, the night before Jesus died. John sets up the story within the drama of Jesus' final time with his disciples:

> Jesus knew that his hour had come to depart from this world and go to the Father. Having loved his own who were in the world, he loved them to the end...
> And during supper Jesus, knowing that the Father had given all things into his hands, and that he had come from God and was going to God, got up from the table, took off his outer robe, and tied a towel around himself. Then he poured water into a basin and began to wash the disciples' feet and to wipe them with the towel that was tied around him.
>
> John 13:1–5

When Jesus came with the bowl to Simon Peter (the same disciple who had fallen on his knees in the boat during the great catch of fish), he was initially refused. Simon Peter could not bear to let Jesus wash his feet. This was the task of a servant, a menial job to cleanse the filth from feet that had been only sandalled during journeys along unpaved roads. Foot washing was surely beneath the man who had performed mighty miracles.

I wonder if some of the impetus for this startling act of intimacy arose from what Jesus had experienced when the woman in our last chapter washed his feet with ointment and tears. Perhaps she had evoked in Jesus the power inherent in such a humble act. More passionately than any words, this visible service could communicate his love for his disciples.

After Jesus had overcome Peter's resistance, and had washed all of their feet, he put on his robe, and went back to the table. Then he spoke to them about the meaning of his action:

> Do you know what I have done to you? You call me Teacher and Lord—and you are right, for that is what I am. So if I, your Lord and Teacher, have washed your feet, you also ought to wash one another's feet. For I have set you an example, that you also should do as I have done to you... Very truly, I tell you, servants are not greater than their master, nor are messengers greater than the one who sent them. If you know these things, you are blessed if you do them.
> John 13:12–17

The repetition in Jesus' words leaves little room for doubt. Three times Jesus told them that they should wash one another's feet. He says it concretely; he gave the literal example to be followed. Of course, further on we will consider this passage in its metaphorical meanings. But first, it is crucial to see that the physical act bears the meaning most effectively. As best as I can read this passage, it seems that Jesus meant us to enact the washing of feet.

The Care of Feet

I have worked with this passage in several groups. Quite consistently, most people are uncomfortable with the thought of literal foot washing. This very resistance can be illuminating.

Before we ever get to actually enacting this ritual, we can understand the quality of relationships Jesus is commanding by exploring what is unsettling in the concrete act. Sticking with the physical dimension of the story before spiritualizing it can reveal the deeper spiritual meanings more clearly.

Recently, the elders in our church studied this passage before going on a retreat that might include a foot washing. They considered the idea of actually doing it. I asked them questions about their preconceptions of what a foot washing would mean: If the thought of foot washing makes you uncomfortable, what in particular do you think creates the difficulty? What quality of relationships is required to enact a ritual so intimate? What would have to change, in you, and in our relationships with one another, in order to make doing this service a greater possibility?

The elders answered candidly with responses such as these: We would need to be vulnerable with each other. We would have to put aside thinking about ourselves for a while to focus on each other. We would have to be courageous; we would have to have faith that God wanted us to do this so we would be able to get through it. We would have to be willing to let our relationships go beneath the surface, to a different level than we usually interact on. We would have to risk being embarrassed in front of each other. We would need love.

On the retreat, enough people had responded favourably for me to risk offering a foot washing ceremony as a voluntary worship service. Right up to the last minute, the bulk of the elders debated participating or not. As the hour came, they decided to risk it.

As we were nervous, we arranged the room to minimize discomfort. Someone lowered the lights. Someone else made sure the doors were shut so passers by would not intrude. Soft music soothed the awkward silences between the sound of splashing water. And then, after reading the passage together, one by one these upper-middle-class, frightened, reserved church elders knelt in front of each other. Shoes were unlaced and gently removed, the precious foot ladled with warm water and towelled off. Twenty minutes passed as each washed and received the washing.

Afterwards, most of them said it was much easier to wash someone's feet than to have their own feet washed. The active washing gave them something to do—maintaining some control over the experience.

But when *your* feet are washed, you can only receive. The warm water and the soft touch feel very good. But it is hard to accept the gift that someone is stooping to bathe your feet, as unique and embarrassing and worn as they may be! When it is over, though, feelings of affection arise. What a tender act, that someone would take off my shoes, rinse, and dry my feet. The experience was humbling for everyone.

The effect was a great release of joy and energy within the group. Our relationships deepened, and a shared commitment to faith grew among the officers. As someone said, 'If we can do that, we can do anything else God asks us!'

Now that we have explored the story literally, what does it say to us symbolically? How will followers of Jesus enact it in everyday life? The meaning of foot washing, of course, goes far deeper than the single act. It becomes a paradigm for relationships between those who are actively reconnecting with God. Washing someone's feet means tending an exposed, humbled part of that person. It means taking gentle care of what is offered to us. All the while, we know that what we are doing is at once very difficult and very comforting for the recipient.

Allowing our feet to be washed means revealing to another person a part of us most often kept hidden and protected. It means risking the sight, smell, and feel of our feet before another person. Effort is needed to receive their ministrations; humility is required to relax enough to be soothed by the gift, as the person washing our feet desires us to be. We are showing a secret side of ourselves and accepting another's care.

It is very difficult to feel superior to someone whose feet you have washed. It is difficult to ignore or put down someone who has recently washed your feet. The interaction between people changes in the glow of such an activity.

Thinking of the story in this way, it becomes

evident what kind of relationships Jesus expected his followers to have. He desires that we relate to one another with increasing openness and honesty. We have noted that our spiritual growth means a greater knowledge of self in concert with a greater knowledge of God; a corresponding exposure of ourselves to others and learning of those others in love completes the picture.

True Community

I have heard the criticism that those who are delving into their personal spiritual growth do so at the expense of concern for others. These critics promote the role of the community of God's people in our development. The story of the foot washing confirms the importance Jesus placed on our relationships not just with God but with others. These are inseparable.

Unfortunately, however, many of us have not experienced meaningful interaction which leads to spiritual growth in the church. Too often churches exhibit what M. Scott Peck has defined as 'pseudo-community'. People get along on the surface. They profess to care for each other; socially they interact. But rarely do the relationships go deeper than ordinary exchanges.

I once asked a woman who had not been to

church for several months if she wouldn't like to come back and join the fellowship. Her reply exposed our pseudo-community all too clearly. She said, 'I've just felt too awful to be with all those happy faces.'

Jesus gave his disciples the ritual of foot washing in order that the church might be a place of tender, intimate care. When hurting people have to put on a smiley face to come to church, somehow we have lost the meaning of foot washing.

The Basement and the Sanctuary

In many churches these days, Twelve Step groups are meeting in basements or tucked away classrooms. These groups are based on the kind of open fellowship inaugurated by Jesus' foot washing. Throughout the course of a meeting, participants share their struggles with alcoholism, food addictions, sexual abuse, or any of many other debilitating behaviours which may be the focus of a particular meeting. The group offers the safety of anonymity to participants, a consistent, uplifting support, and an understanding forgiveness of failures. In addition, these fellowships refer to the Twelve Steps[1], a list of principles which includes a firm reliance on a Higher Power to transform those aspects of life over which we are powerless.

The Twelve Step groups are attempting to live out the very kind of spirituality we have been describing in these pages. The Christians who worship upstairs in the sanctuaries could learn quite a bit from their partners in the basement. At the same time, participants in Twelve Step groups have provided the inspiration for this work. Many have told me they long for more spiritual meat than their meetings provide. They desire to re-enter Christian faith, and discover how the stories of Jesus relate to their new-found honesty and vulnerability.

Both groups could learn from each other. How wonderful it would be if the basement and the sanctuary were brought closer together. I am hopeful that Jesus' gift of the foot washing ritual can be recovered, at both the literal and symbolic level to help us move in that direction.

Foot washing

Reconnecting with God is an intensely personal activity. Much of it has to be done alone. We need enough silence to hear what God, and our deepest selves, may be saying. Space apart from the demands of the world is necessary for us to get in touch with our yearning for God and to make our way home.

At the same time, we cannot reconnect without other people. God has made us to interact with one another. For many, confession can only occur if there is a ready ear to hear. Some need the help of others to make sense of their thoughts, to sort out their feelings. Most of us benefit from direction in the interpretation of Bible stories. Many of the moments crucial to my own growth have occurred in conversations of foot washing quality with other people.

As you grow in your relationship to God, it is essential to be in conversation with other people on a similar journey. We need each other to keep up our courage, to expose our rationalizations, and to affirm our progress. We worship, not only in private, but together with other followers of Jesus. We study, not just alone, but with others to gain new perspectives and share our unique insights.

So I will recommend to you that you get involved in a church if you are not already. I will say straightforwardly that, once in a church, many of your interactions might be disappointing. Our churches are full of pseudo-community and full of people who are frightened to take the stories of Jesus personally and seriously. The fact that you are consciously on a spiritual quest makes you different from the majority of people. A certain amount of loneliness can be expected.

At the same time, God never leaves us alone.

There are people in every place who make it a priority to live in tune with God. In fact, as you awaken more and more to the spiritual life, you will find those people on a similar journey, as if they are appearing from nowhere. Where once you thought you were alone, soon you will find help in the most unexpected places.

God will meet our needs for spiritual interaction with others.

Jesus' command of foot washing, though, makes some requirements of us as well. Reconnecting with God is not an activity for our benefit alone. We may decide we can live with misery on certain days and simply not pursue serving God. After all, 'It's my life.'

But the truth is that others are depending on us to move along in our journeys so that we may be of some aid to them.

Those who take Jesus' command of foot washing seriously will look for tired, hurting feet among those they meet. Not just literally, of course. But as we listen and grow more sensitive, we can apprehend when others are hurting. Many will expose a bit of their pain to see how we respond. We can grow in our ability to make inquiries about other people's lives. The basin of warm water to soothe aching muscles is offered every time we ask to listen to another person's story. Our compassion is a soft towel as we treat another person's feet, their exposed and embarrassing aspects, as a precious treasure.

Along the way of following Jesus, we will try to deepen the interactions we have with other people. We can take the risk by exposing more of ourselves than we usually do. So to speak, we can offer our feet. Every interaction is a chance for showing forth love. Many encounters include an opportunity to take the conversation deeper. We can practice going down into the ache of life instead of always trying to be 'up' in the forced hilarity of our culture.

This is not a book about the art of learning to love. Many chapters could be written about the practice of foot washing. I can recommend two that will be of great help: Morton Kelsey's *Caring*, and M. Scott Peck's *The Road Less Travelled*.

For now, it is enough to see in this story that Jesus requires his followers to practice the same kind of confession and compassion with each other as we have experienced with him. In conclusion, we can note as well that our close connection with Jesus is what makes this kind of loving possible. Alone, just trying to be good, we may often lack the courage for foot washing. But our service grows from our connection to the source.

The heart of God was revealed in this foot

washing. During the night when the powers of darkness were riding the winds, when urgency would have driven most of us to frenzy, Jesus slowly, deliberately washed the feet of each disciple. When he had only one evening left to teach them the essence of his desire for them, Jesus washed his disciples' feet.

In a coming chapter we will explore more fully what Jesus' exposure of himself means to us. Now we see that whenever we would turn away from this risk with others, we can draw strength from Jesus' own action, and his words, 'So if I, your Lord and Teacher, have washed your feet, you also ought to wash one another's feet.'

Questions for Reflection

The story of the foot washing is found in John 13:1–20.

1) What are some ways, besides literally, that we both wash other people's feet and have our feet washed?

2) How would you say Jesus has washed your feet?

3) What in your experience of the love of Jesus forms the basis for washing others' feet?

4) How does this kind of service link us to Christ? What would need to change in our relationships with others in order to make enacting a foot washing a greater possibility?

5) How have aspects of the church blocked the quality of relationship demanded by foot washing?

6) In churches you have seen, what activities, structures, programmes, or attitudes help to promote relationships of 'foot washing' quality?

7) Who are the people in your life with whom you come closest to having this kind of relationship? What new risks of love might you be called to take as a result of your spiritual growth?

Exercises

1) Conduct a week long experiment during which time you will try to note where in conversations you could take things to a deeper level. Try, if you are able, in compassion to make inquiries about another's life, to risk going down into pain and avoid only going up into superficiality. Each evening make notes on your progress, the reactions of others, and the degree of risk required.

2) If you are in a study group, consider conducting a foot washing. I have seen it work well when the group first reads and discusses the passage. We usually arrange chairs in a circle and play a tape of soft, meditative music. Then, working with two basins and towels, the first two participants kneel before two others. We stress that anyone has the right to decline participation simply by shaking their head if someone comes to them. If there is agreement, however, the foot washers take off the shoes of the ones sitting. Then, with first one foot and then the other over the bowl, the washer ladles the feet with warm water. Then the washers towel off the feet and pass the towel to the one sitting, going back to their own chairs. This continues until everyone has washed once and been washed once.

3) Read the following prayer from Origen, the third-century theologian and Father of the Church:

> Jesus, come, my feet are dirty. You have become a servant for my sake, so fill your basin with water; come, wash my feet. I know that I am bold in saying this, but your own words have made me fearful: 'If I do not wash your feet, you will

have no companionship with me.' Wash my feet, then, so that I may be your companion. But what am I saying, 'Wash my feet'? Peter could say these words, for all that needed washing were his feet. For the rest, he was completely clean. I must be made clean with that other washing of which you said: 'I have a baptism with which I must be baptized.'[2]

Notes

[1] Both Gerald May and Keith Miller have done excellent work linking addiction and recovery to Christian spirituality. I recommend especially Gerald May, *The Awakened Heart*, HarperSan Francisco, 1991, and Keith Miller, *Hope in the Fast Lane*, Harper & Row, San Francisco, 1987.

[2] Translated by Agnes Cunningham in Gabe Huck and Mary Anne Simcoe, editors, *A Triduum Sourcebook*, Liturgy Training Publications, Chicago, 1983, page 10

~8~

The Face That Is Everywhere

THE LAST PUBLIC TEACHING OF JESUS RECORDED IN the Gospel of Matthew is a provocative parable about the criteria God will use for judgment. He said that at the end of time he would be seated on a throne of glory. All people will be gathered before him. And then, with the authority of a king and the job of a shepherd, Jesus will separate people into two groups, the sheep and the goats. To the ones designated as sheep, the king will set forth his reasons for a good judgment:

> Come, you that are blessed by my Father, inherit the kingdom prepared for you from the foundation of the world; for I was hungry and you gave me food, I was thirsty and you gave me something to drink, I was a stranger and you welcomed me, I was naked and you gave me clothing, I was sick and you took care of me, I was in prison and you visited me.
>
> Matthew 25:34–37

With a repetition of the entire list, the righteous will inquire about when they had ever seen their Lord in such states as hunger or imprisonment. And Jesus said he will make the startling reply, 'Truly I tell you, just as you did it to one of the least of these who are members of my family, you did it to me.'

In the parable, the king will go on to curse the unrighteous for failing to give him drink, to welcome him, to clothe him and so on. They, in shock at their offence, will ask when they could ever have been guilty of such horrible neglect. The answer will be chilling, 'Truly I tell you, just as you did not do it to one of the least of these, you did not do it to me.'

I imagine that the context of eternal judgment in this parable will make quite a few readers uncomfortable. The whole issue of the wrath and justice of a loving God is an important one.

We will touch on it in the next chapter, hopefully enough to satisfy the most immediate questions. Our subject, though, is not the last judgment but what Jesus asks of us in this present life.

The force of this parable actually concerns the way we live now; doctrine about afterlife is not its focus. Parables are meant to inspire a change in thought or action as they are told. We will see that this story of Jesus can provide a strong source for energizing and focusing our lives.

In the account of the foot washing, Jesus repeated his command three times that the disciples wash one another's feet. Given the economical writing style of the Bible, such repetition signals an important and unmistakable imperative. In this parable of the sheep and goats, Jesus repeated his list four times. There could be no doubt in his audience of what he was trying to say.

When we give food to someone who is hungry, we are giving it to Jesus. If we ignore someone who is thirsty, we have denied Jesus a drink. Welcoming a stranger with open arms is embracing our Lord himself. But sizing up persons, dismissing their importance, and turning away are equivalent to dispensing with Jesus.

Jesus left us with an ethic for meaningful and personal social action. The church has followed his intent in its history of ministries of compassion. As we grow in being followers of Jesus, we discover that our relationship to Jesus includes care of the least of these; if we want to touch him, to be near him, to show love for him, we do so or fail to do so by our actions toward the least.

At first this may seem overwhelming. Indeed this is one of the most challenging of his teachings. It's exhausting to think that soon there will be nearly five billion people on earth. If all of them are, in effect, Jesus, and if any of them is in need, I am hopelessly behind and doomed to be one of the goats. This parable becomes not motivating but humiliating.

Several important considerations, however, can help us turn this teaching around into a well-spring for replenishing our acts of compassion. First, we may understand that the parable uses hyperbole. The force of its message was to wake us up to the reality that the least little one is worthy of care; in the most obscure and undesirable, there is Jesus waiting to be loved.

Of course we cannot succeed every time; God knows that we cannot be perfect. We do not instantly become 'goats' because of our past or even future neglects. The parable is intended to motivate us now to begin seeing others with the same affection we have for Jesus.

Secondly, we may realize that not every person in the world is or can be our responsibility. To be sure, many of us are not acting on behalf of others anywhere near our capacity. Some are overworked and approaching burnout. In a lecture on healing and love, Morton Kelsey, the author and priest who exhibits a rich compassion to all he encounters made this observation. He likened our call to love to picking up bundles. No one can pick up all the bundles in the world. The key is to find those bundles with our names on them. We strive to discern which people are our bundles and which are not. When we are comfortable that we are tending to the bundles God has given us, we may leave the rest in God's care.[1]

Thirdly, considering the 'least of these' as if they were Jesus need not make us feel guilty that we do not love them more. Rather, we may use this idea to fuel our imaginations and thereby inspire our love. If we have met Jesus in the story of the woman at the well, we have felt love swell in us for this one who knows us so well and loves us anyway. In the story of the rich man, we may have felt relief that Jesus does not mean for us to play the world's game and succeed in all the wrong places. We can love him with our whole heart. The sinful woman found forgiveness, and entering that story, we too may have felt the healing of old wounds. In all these stories, Jesus elicits love from us. He draws us to him; his compassion sparks our devotion. We may transfer our feelings of affection for Jesus onto those in the world whom we would otherwise consider least. Our love for Jesus can lead us. By loving them, we are loving him. Visiting the sick suddenly becomes a romantic thing to do— this is Jesus whom I adore lying there.

Who are the least of Jesus' family? My interpretation of this passage is that he means everyone. The Christian belief is that God became a human being in Jesus. God was wrapped in flesh in the person of Christ. By entering the world, taking on our state, sharing the kinship of all flesh, God in Jesus became brother to all people.

The least to us may range broadly. Of course the faraway poor come to mind, those who are strangers to our Western comforts and economies. They are also much closer to home. The least is the person whom other people avoid. At work there is some 'least of these' who perhaps bears the brunt of coffee hour chatter. The least show up in churches as the ones who are too obviously needy of attention, too vocal, too different from the rest. Families may spawn someone who becomes the least of these, as an object of blame for the family's problems.

We can be honest enough to admit that the least of these for us personally are probably the people we 'least' want to be around.

I was raised with a Dutch Calvinist fear of hospitals and sick people. Surely if someone with a physical handicap touches me, I will catch it! Loud, abrasive people become the least for me; I steer around them as much as possible, unless I can think of a safe, anonymous way to deflate them. Elderly people and children alike can become least when they require care, when they are at a stage in life that requires more intake than they can pay for with output. There are people on the streets and in certain areas with whom I fear contact. I do not know what to say to their pain; I have no solutions to their poverty. They are the least of these, and I can't seem to help it. The least are all over the place, wherever people are reduced, dismissed, shunned, or avoided.

The raw truth is that many people who feel undesirable to us will always seem that way. Obnoxious people more than likely will be obnoxious. Sick people will not stop being ill just so we can have an easier time visiting them. Prisoners will not often have troubled pasts transformed into bright futures. Some people will always be scary. It takes a long time for misfits to fit.

A life which is reconnected with God through our encounters with Jesus needs to find expression of Christ's compassion in order to stay connected. We have seen throughout this study that God pours forth love to heal us, but not to sit idle and grow stagnant within us. God's love is meant to flow through us to others. As Jesus offers us so much life, he also asks us to respond, with a dedication of our lives to following him and a new intention to relate to others with compassion. We seek to develop relationships of foot washing intimacy. But what about the least of these?

We can begin to look at others with a spiritually romantic imagination. Knowing full well that the person is not ontologically, literally Jesus, we pretend. I look at the one in the bed and say, 'There is Jesus. I love Jesus, and so I will love this one.' The loud person goes into his needy tirade. Instead of turning away, I can use imagination. There is Jesus; he is lonesome and needy in that person. I can speak to him.

Amazingly, looking in this way, we begin to see people differently. The least are elevated from that dreadful category. It is a moving experience to suddenly see in the incoherent expression of a woman in a nursing home the Christ who has loved me so much. She gains more worth in my perception than I would have thought possible, and so my attitude and actions toward her change as well. And it is not by guilty, straining compulsion, but through the joyful romance of my feelings for Jesus.

All our efforts at spiritual deepening are not merely for ourselves. Reconnecting with God is the only way I have found to gain an ethic for social action not based on guilt. It is the only way I know to find energy instead of burnout. A needy world is waiting for people who have the enthusiasm for compassion and the creativity for service inspired by a personal love for Jesus.

And, of course, our spiritual lives will cease to progress without working on the outward expression of the inner life. After a certain level, spiritual development requires this external focus. Attempting to love and do good works without a connection to the source of love eventually burns us out; we wake in the middle of the night and wonder why we keep on being good when so little seems to come of it. The source and motivation comes from seeing that what we do to the least, we do to Jesus. So he, not an ideal, not guilt, not duty, not anything but Christ himself becomes the beginning point of all our actions.

Overcoming Difficulty

Sometimes our imaginations may flag at seeing Jesus in some people. The violence, the self-centredness, the distortions of addiction may daunt us. We may feel that the person of Jesus and the forcefully apparent characteristics of the least of these are in contradiction. We know mentally that we are called to treat each one as we would treat Jesus, whom we have grown to love. But no love is being inspired in us.

In such times, I have found it helpful to reverse the imagery. I strive not to see Jesus in the person, but to see the person through Jesus' eyes. He was able to deal with self-righteous Pharisees, people possessed by demons, lepers, weasels in business, the persistent, and all kinds of needy people like us. So, if I can link myself with the stories of Jesus' interactions with people, I can be moved along with compassion.

Riding up the elevator to visit someone gravely ill, I may be suddenly struck with the force of my background. I am repulsed. There is no way I can go and smell that disease, or look at the feeding tube, or clasp that limp hand. I want to slip a card under the door and run. But sometimes, I can lay hold of a story of Jesus and find strength.

Jesus did not turn away from the man who had lived among the tombs. That man was bruised with open sores, naked, unwashed, and howling. Jesus received him and made him well. In the name of that Jesus I will go into this room and receive the ill one whom I find.

An ancient prayer attributed to St Patrick attempts to bind the person who prays with the life of Jesus:

I bind unto myself today
The strong name of the Trinity.
. . . .
I bind this day to me for ever,
By power of faith, Christ's incarnation,
His baptism in the Jordan River,
His death on cross for my salvation.

We grasp hold of some aspect of Jesus' life and assume it as ours when we know that we will need strength for showing compassion to the least.

For example, I may be preparing for an encounter with someone I detest because he refuses to examine his life, he consistently avoids being responsible for his growth, and then wonders why he has so many problems. It is helpful then to remember the woman at the well. 'I bind unto myself this day, Jesus' talking to the woman along his way; he did not turn from her chequered past; he offered her drink which would last.' Remembering the story, I claim Jesus' compassion as my own.

Again we see the connection between personal spiritual growth and effective action in the world. When I learn and practise recalling the stories of Jesus, I have new sources to enable me to minister to the least of these. The story of the feeding of the five thousand when Jesus was tired and wanted to be alone, may revive me when I resent the ignorance that has brought people to the soup kitchen. His confrontations with the Pharisees may help me know that the kindest thing I can do in a situation is to be honest. The list goes on and on, but the principle is the same.

We are called to show compassion to others as if each one were Jesus. Such a spiritual connection motivates and elicits our love when we use a spiritual romantic imagination.

Questions for Reflection

The parable of the sheep and goats is found in Matthew 25:31–46.

1) What does it mean to be one of the 'least'?

2) In what situations do you often find Jesus hungry, sick, in prison, a stranger, naked, and thirsty? Can you name the least who are in your community? your church? your workplace or school? your family?

3) What is annoying about the least? What don't you like about them?

4) How could thinking of each of the least as being Jesus help your interaction with them?

5) Why do you think Jesus was so serious about this?

Exercises

1) Close your eyes and wait quietly for some of the 'least of these' whom you have encountered recently to appear in your mind. See them there. See Jesus in each one. Ask yourself then, 'What concrete expression of compassion could I perform for each one of these? Can I imagine doing it out of love for Jesus? Am I willing to do it?'

2) The Celtic tradition of prayer has an excellent history of seeing God in all things and seeing Christ in others. Try these prayers:

Christmas Poor

You are the caller
You are the poor
You are the stranger at my door

You are the wanderer
The unfed
You are the homeless
With no bed

You are the man
Driven insane
You are the child
Crying in pain

You are the other who comes to me
If I open to another, you're born in me

Thou Art God

Thou art the peace of all things calm
Thou art the place to hide from harm
Thou art the light that shines in dark
Thou art the heart's eternal spark
Thou art the door that's open wide
Thou art the guest that waits inside
Thou art the stranger at the door
Thou art the calling of the poor
Thou art my Lord and with me still
Thou art my love, keep me from ill
Thou art the light, the truth, the way
Thou art my Saviour this very day.

Celtic Rune of Hospitality

I saw a stranger yestreen,
I put food in the eating place,
drink in the drinking place,

music in the listening place,
and in the sacred name of the Triune,
He blessed myself and my house,
my cattle and my dear ones,
and the lark said in her song
Often, often, often,
goes the Christ in the stranger's guise.[2]

Kenneth MacLeod, Iona Community

Notes

[1] Morton Kelsey, from a lecture on healing given at Stony Point Conference Centre, New York, May, 1988.

[2] From an Iona Community postcard, Kenneth MacLeod.

~9~

The Cup of Blessing

WE HAVE BEEN CONSIDERING SEVERAL STORIES OF Jesus—parables he told and accounts of his interactions with people. All along we have been listening for what Jesus offers to those whom he encounters. And we have searched for what he asks of those who decide to follow him. Our goal has been to re-enter the Gospel stories and discover if we can find our lives there. Hopefully, in the characters we have met, we have found some fresh ways to help us reconnect to God.

Now we will turn to the meaning of Jesus' life and death as a whole. First, we will consider his death on the cross, then, in the next chapter, his resurrection. Again, I hope we can make our approach from within the stories. Rather than being outside observers or theological commentators, we will try to creep up on the edges of two crucial events and catch a glimpse from the inside out.

The death of Jesus is one of the central themes of Christian faith, yet also one of the most difficult. From the beginning, Christians have believed that when Jesus went to the cross, he took our sins upon himself. Somehow, his death was for us. He died for our sins. The prophecy of Isaiah was fulfilled, 'Surely he hath borne our griefs, and carried our sorrows... He was wounded for our transgressions, he was bruised for our iniquities... and with his stripes we are healed... the Lord hath laid on him the iniquity of us all' (Isaiah 53:4–6, KJV).

In the ancient way of thinking, one person could be the representative for many; one willing victim could be a substitute for another. Our sins warranted God's punishment; Jesus offered himself in our place, thus cancelling the debt we owed to God and making possible the forgiveness of our sins. By his death, we were made right with God.

I believe in this doctrine of Christianity, classically called 'substitutionary atonement'. I also find that when I try to comprehend it, let alone explain it, the words swirl around and my thoughts are muddied. It is very difficult to grasp how one could give his life for the rest of us.

Moreover, I am aware that many people have even less success than I do in making sense of the death of Jesus. Some are horrified with the idea that God has wrath towards the world that needs to be turned away. Others feel that this concept is too much like a financial transaction: Jesus paid for your sins, now trade your allegiance to him for that forgiveness, and the deal is done.

A dear friend recently pinpointed his difficulty:

> I can experience Jesus as quite real because he incarnated the essence of God, which then became available for us; and once you're in touch with that essence, you're no longer caught in the world of sin... [But] I have never been able to do anything with the theological construction that Jesus suffered for our sins and functioned as a sort of surrogate scapegoat. It never made sense to me, never touched me, either mythologically or historically.

Such doubts are significant. We may not ignore the questions that plague so many. Neither may we dispense with Jesus' crucifixion because its importance is difficult to understand.

I am hopeful that we can explore the death of Jesus in this chapter in a way that will allow its meaning to open up for us. We will return again to the last meal Jesus shared with his disciples, and then follow him into the Garden of Gethsemane where he prayed shortly before his arrest. We will focus on the image, not of the cross, but of the cup, as our way in. Through this back door, I hope we will gain entrance to the meaning of his death before the fact.

The Cup

On his last night with his disciples, perhaps before he washed their feet, Jesus celebrated the traditional Jewish feast of Passover with them. Passover was the most sacred of all religious rituals. The people gathered with their families in their homes to recall the story of how God had set them free from slavery in Egypt. Every aspect of the meal, each item of food and drink, was part of the formal ritual.[1]

There were four cups of wine to be shared during the course of the feast. These four cups corresponded to the four parts of a promise God gave to Israel while still in captivity. As the meal progressed, the head of the family raised the cup and recited a prayer. Then the cup would be shared as the promise was recalled.

Some biblical scholars have concluded that Jesus broke into the ritual with his own words about the meaning of the meal during the passing of the third cup, the cup of redemption.[2] The third part of God's promise was 'I will redeem you with an outstretched arm and mighty acts of judgment' (Exodus 6:6). This cup recalled how the Hebrews, groaning under the hot sun in their service to the Pharaoh, were set free after God had sent ten terrible plagues.

God parted the waters of the Red Sea for the fleeing Hebrews, then closed the waters over the pursuing Egyptians. By a mighty act, God's people were liberated, but their oppressors were destroyed. The cup of redemption for the Hebrews was a cup of judgment for the Egyptians.

It was at this point in the recollection that Jesus interrupted the traditional order and added his own words about the cup. Looking at the red wine remaining in the goblet he said, 'This cup is the new covenant in my blood which is poured out for you.' The cup of judgment became the cup of Jesus' blood poured out. In the Passover meal, the judgment of God was described as the destruction of the Egyptian army. Now we are to think of God's act of judgment as the offering of Jesus' life.

In the Garden

After supper, Jesus went into the Garden of Gethsemane to pray, and the image of the cup recurred. Jesus went a little way ahead of his disciples, fell to his knees and prayed, 'Father, for you all things are possible; remove this cup from me; yet, not what I want, but what you want.' Luke records that Jesus was in 'anguish' and 'he prayed more earnestly, and his sweat became like great drops of blood falling down on the ground'.

Within the story, the cup seemed to represent Jesus' fate or destiny, simply that which would befall him. Drinking the cup would mean accepting the path before him; refusing the cup would be resisting his destiny and trying to turn aside from the direction God had given him. The cup was that future course offered to him by God.

We know that Jesus knew the Hebrew scriptures. I wonder, as he prayed, if Jesus recalled any of the times when 'cup' had been used in the past. Surely he knew by heart the sixteenth psalm, which includes this line, 'The Lord is my portion and my cup.' That portion which befell the psalmist in life was God himself. Jesus knew, too, of Psalm 23, 'Thou anointest my head with oil, my cup runneth over' (KJV). The cup represents one's very life, which can overflow with the presence of the Lord. The cup in these psalms was one's lot in life, what was given to one by God. For the psalm writer, that cup was one of joy and love, for God was the cup itself.

In the Old Testament, there is another shade to the meaning of the cup, one not so bright with hope. The cup is still what one receives from God, but in Psalm 60, the writer's vessel is filled with 'the wine of astonishment' (KJV). The prophet Isaiah wrote, 'Stand up, O Jerusalem, you who have drunk at the hand of the Lord the cup of his wrath, you who have drunk to the dregs the bowl of staggering' (Isaiah 51:17).

These passages evoke a cup bubbling over with destruction. What is given from the Lord is judgment for a rebellious people who had forgotten the poor and forgotten the Lord. If Jesus associated the cup he was about to drink with this cup, then perhaps he felt he would soon be draining a bowl full of wrath. The cup of judgment led to suffering. And Jesus prayed that he might be spared such a cup.

This was not merely wishful thinking. There was yet another scriptural reference to the cup which might have awakened this hope. In the same chapter of Isaiah, we read, 'See I have taken from your hand the cup of staggering; you shall drink no more from the bowl of my wrath.' God who gave the cup could also take it away.

Before studying these uses of *cup* in the Old Testament, I had never known that Jesus had any hope of getting out of his imminent suffering. It pierces me to imagine him in prayer, recalling these words of Isaiah, and wondering if he might yet be spared a painful death. There was a flicker of hope for him even as he knew there was no hope.

Have you ever known this feeling? Perhaps in the moment when a relationship was moving toward an inevitable end, you have felt your heart catch with the thought, 'But it's not over yet. Could we try again?' Even as you thought it, even as the hope arose, it died. The end is the end.

This instant of hope in the garden was like the drive to the vet when you almost turn the car around, and say to yourself, 'I'll take care of him; he'll get over the pain and everything will be fine.' But you know you have to drive on.

This is the afternoon when, walking up the stairs, before you catch yourself, you start to think of what you will say to the one who is no longer there.

As I feel with this moment in the Garden, I wonder if God's heart wasn't broken to hear that hope rise in Jesus. Didn't God want to spare him then, to let the world go to hell if only he could save Jesus the pain? How did God ever turn away from that prayer?

Jesus was about to drink a cup of wrath. The idea of God's judgment is hard for us these days. We wonder why there is so much wrath in the Bible when our religion is supposed to be about a loving God. There is no escaping it. From Genesis through to Revelation, including the Psalms that we cherish and the words of Jesus we love, judgment is a part of God.

How are we to understand this cup of wrath before Jesus? It seems to me that wrath is not a primary emotion, but a secondary one. Anger is the result of something else. Wrath may arise from offence. When one's sense of what is right is violated, anger occurs. Even more, wrath may be derived from pain, either feared or experienced, for oneself or for others. The very angry person is a very pained one. Perhaps deeply scarred by a terrible wrong or threatened by an uprooting change, or finding our children in harm's way, we may be roused to a ferocious anger. Anger is a reaction of protection and may be an expression of love when the loved one faces harm.

So, if wrath is born of pain, what pain has God known to have such anger kindled? What pain of God was poured into the goblet of wrath which Jesus drank?

147

I do not believe it was merely pain caused when someone deducted a dubious business trip on a tax return. Nor is the goblet overfilled because someone let slip a swear-word in traffic and another had a few too many at the Christmas party. We can too easily be full of our petty mistakes, hiding from God as from a headmaster who lives to catch students in menial sins.

All the while I am wrapped in my little worries, a boy looks with dismay and incomprehension as a parent walks out the door. 'It's not your fault,' he is told, but he still believes it is, years later. Children cry in hunger and others call the problem politics, mumbling things such as, 'Those people need to get a work ethic.' Every other week it seems that oil spills into the waters, fouling everything from our creeks to the oceans. But it is not economical to build tankers which cannot be punctured with a pin.

In our world, species disappear, rain forests burn, innocent people are cheated, wars continue, and arms are sold to anyone with cash. This kind of list could go on for volumes.

We see the pain of the world, and even we are outraged. As narcissistic as I am most of the time, the suffering in the world can still move me to wrath. And if we get angry, do you think God, who loves so much more than we, also gets angry? The wrath of God is surely kindled by the suffering we cause one another, wrath enough to reduce the world to cinders if something did not contain it—if Jesus had not drunk to the dregs the goblet of God's wrath over all we have done.

In the Garden, there was a cup of wrath to be drunk. Anger piqued by the pain of the world had to be assuaged. The scriptures portray God as full of wrath; we are told God will judge with good reason. But, thankfully, there is a deeper essence to God. Wrath is secondary to pain, and pain arises from love. God is love. As someone said, 'At the centre of the universe, there beats a heart of love.'

In the same scriptures that describe the wrath of God, we also see God pulling back the anger, taking the wrath onto himself, bearing the tremendous price of setting us free. God forgives.

In the story of Jesus in the Garden, we see that the cup of judgment was not poured out onto the world in destruction. Rather, Jesus drank it. The cup he drank, taking wrath into himself, becomes for us the cup of blessing. The cup of judgment becomes the cup of salvation. This is what Jesus proclaimed at the Passover supper, chose in the Garden, and endured in his death.

Here is the mightiest of the mighty acts of God: wrapped in flesh, incarnate in Jesus, God drinks his own cup of wrath, deep within, to the point of death.

And so, in the Garden, instead of passing the cup, walking away to leave us to fend for ourselves, Jesus looked at the bubbling bowl and said in his prayer, 'Yet, not my will but yours be done.' The Greek word translated as 'yet' can also be rendered as 'nevertheless'. This is a word which bespeaks a turning point in intention. 'Father, take this cup, *nevertheless*, not my will but yours be done.' Nevertheless. He spoke the word into the dark night of a world in pain. Nevertheless. He spoke the word into the silent wrath of God's turned back. Nevertheless. 'I will take the cup; I will drink the goblet.'

What the Cup Means for Us

Jesus enacted just what he required of those whom he encountered. He asked the rich man to sell all he had; he asked the fishermen to leave their nets and follow him; he accepted the outpouring of the woman's grief, her vulnerability as the faith which led to forgiveness and a new life. In the Garden Jesus offered his life to be handed over to death because it was his cup, the will of God for him. Jesus embraced the paradox of all spirituality: to save one's life, it must be lost. He did it literally.

God took on the responsibility of caring for the pain of the world by entering it in Jesus. Rather than turn away in exasperation to leave us in the chaos we created, God waded right into the mess. Jesus was not insulated from the people around him; he walked among us, he was vulnerable. He drew to himself the pain and hate of the world. Sins were forgiven; illnesses were healed. When the jealousy of those who hated him turned to violence, he did not resist, but received it all. He embraced the world unto death.

It is as if he said, 'In this life there is suffering and death; evil befalls, and I will not turn from that. Though I could save myself, I will not. I will receive the hatred and rage, torture and rejection of a world in pain.

'I go before you. I will undergo all you suffer and have experienced. None of your life will be foreign to me. You will know always that wherever you have been, I have been also. Because I go through death and come out living again, you are no longer captive to death. Because I take the sin and the rage of the world fully upon myself, receiving it in my body, and come out the other side, you are no longer captive to your sin and rage. You are not left alone. I have been through it all before you; I walk with you through life and death now.'

Because Jesus has gone before us, and has

turned the cup of wrath into a cup of blessing, we are free to face our lives. We are free to look at all the pain which has been inflicted upon us and no longer be overwhelmed with debilitating shame. All the sickness which has diminished us, all the pathology which has damaged us need no longer rule us.

And, in turn, we are free to face all the pain we have inflicted on others, and know that we may stop. We may receive grace; we may begin to set things right.

Jesus has drunk the cup. We need no longer live under the wrath which leads to destruction and bitterness. I do not have the experience in suffering to say to one in pain, 'Give up your anger and find the deeper healing of God's love.' My suffering has not been sufficient to withstand the retort, 'You do not know what I have been through.' No, I do not know. But Jesus knows. He has known trouble in his soul unto death, agony of decision unto sweating drops of blood, pain in his body beyond the limits of mortal enduring, and utter humiliation of his gracious offers of love.

And he declares that we may let our pain go. Someone has paid for all this trouble. There is peace the other side of owning and giving over our rage to Jesus. There is healing the other side of owning and giving over our destructive ways of living to Christ. There is joy the other side of owning and giving over guilt and bitterness and failure to him. We may pour it all into his cup. He will drink it. We can let it go. Someone has paid for all this trouble. Judgment has become redemption. Jesus has drunk the cup of the world's pain to the dregs.

Our Part

There is one more piece to the death of Jesus for us to consider. Jesus expected that his followers would also drink the cup. He knew that whoever loved him would have to take a road that led through death to new life. 'If any want to become my followers, let them deny themselves and take up their cross and follow me. For those who want to save their life will lose it, and those who lose their life for my sake... will save it.'

The Gospels record numerous predictions by Jesus of his death at the hands of the religious authorities and his subsequent resurrection. He knew what he was getting into. Once, shortly after one of these predictions, two of the disciples asked if they could sit with Jesus when he came into his heavenly glory. They had missed the part about suffering altogether. Jesus ended up telling them, 'The cup that I drink you will drink.'

Then he said, 'whoever wishes to be great among you must be your servant, and whoever wishes to be first among you must be the slave of all. For the Son of Man came not to be served but to serve and to give his life as a ransom for many.'

This is the way I hear his voice, 'You too will suffer with me, will lose yourselves if you are to be my followers. This is the way of the kingdom. This is the essence of who I am and what I am doing here. I lay down my life from beginning to end in love.

'I am the healer; I am the binder of wounds; I am the forgiver of sins; I am the embracer of outcasts. I am also death. I am death to the life that does not belong to God. I am death to anything but living life wholeheartedly for the sake of God's little ones. I go to my death. You must follow as you are required.

'This is the way of God; I must suffer, and give my life for the ransom of many. I take your pain unto myself. I hug your diseases and make them whole. I bear your sins in my body as I hang on the cross.

'But more, oh more. You will go where I go. You are to live with the cross on your back. You will drink the cup I drink. If you would be mine, every day, every hour, devote your life to me; embrace these little ones who seem not to count. Every day be the servant. Deny yourself for the sake of your Lord and his children.'

Jesus understood his death as fitting naturally with his life, with the work that he did. He did not turn from it. What's more, he considered his death to be what we pass through to be his followers.

Now I don't care much for this. It demands my very life. T.S. Eliot wrote, 'And the time of death is every moment.'[3] Following Jesus is a continual giving up of the old, egocentric, dysfunctional lives we have led. Fortunately, there is a new life constantly offered as a substitute. We are not left in the Garden; resurrection will follow.

Questions for Discussion and Reflection

The story of the cup is found in Mark 14:22–42.

1) What thoughts have you had about the apparent contradiction between the love of God and the wrath of God?

2) How is Jesus God's answer to the pain of the world and the wrath of God?

3) What do you understand the death of Jesus to mean?

4) Jesus said in an act of consecration, 'Nevertheless, not my will but your will be done.' How might that statement be applied to our spiritual lives?

5) What would you like to pour into the cup which Jesus drank?

6) What could it mean in your relationships to discover that Jesus has already suffered for the pain you have experienced and caused?

Exercises

1) Write down several memories, emotions, or habits you wish could put into Jesus' cup.

2) Using rich colours from crayons or markers, draw the cup which Jesus drank; allow it to contain the mistakes, the pain, the sin, and the suffering which you need to pour in at this time.

   Discuss with a partner or in a journal your reactions when you are finished. Perhaps offer this cup to Jesus in prayer.

3) Practice this meditative exercise, preferably in a group setting: Visualize Jesus sitting at a table, inviting you to come and sit before him. In the

centre of the table is a chalice full of dark wine. He tells you that this is the cup he has chosen to drink; it is a cup of the world's pain and rage. He invites you to put your pain, your rage, your guilt, your sorrow into the cup and allow him to drink it. He very much wants these from you.

Imagine yourself pouring in the emotions and the memories. See him taking them from you in his cup, and then drinking it down. When he is finished, he slides the cup across the table and invites you to drink it now. 'This is my blood, which is poured out for you and for many for the forgiveness of sins.' See yourself drain the cup and feel its contents fill you. When you have finished, Jesus embraces you and sends you back to your life.

Debrief this exercise with a partner; make notes in a journal.

4) Meditate on this prayer from T.S. Eliot's 'East Coker'.

> The wounded surgeon plies the steel
> That questions the distempered part;
> Beneath the bleeding hands we feel
> The sharp compassion of the healer's art
> Resolving the enigma of the fever chart.

Our only health is the disease
If we obey the dying nurse
Whose constant care is not to please
But to remind of our, and Adam's curse,
And that, to be restored, our sickness must
    grow worse.

The whole earth is our hospital
Endowed by the ruined millionaire,
Wherein, if we do well, we shall
Die of the absolute paternal care
That will not leave us, but prevents us
    everywhere.
. . . .

The dripping blood our only drink,
The bloody flesh our only food:
In spite of which we like to think
That we are sound, substantial flesh and
    blood—
Again, in spite of that, we call this Friday
    good.[4]

Notes

[1] William L. Lane, *The Gospel of Mark*, William B. Eerdmans Publishing Company, Grand Rapids, 1974, pages 504–13. Lane gives an excellent commentary on the relationship between the Passover and the Last Supper.

[2] Barbara Balzac Thompson, *Passover Seder*, Augsburg Publishing House, Minneapolis, 1984. A complete menu and detailed order of the ritual are provided.

[3] T.S. Eliot, 'The Dry Salvages' from *Four Quartets*, Faber and Faber, London, 1944, page 36

[4] T.S. Eliot, 'East Coker' from *Four Quartets*, Faber and Faber, London, 1944, pages 25–26

~10~

Burning Hearts

FORTUNATELY, DYING SYMBOLICALLY WITH JESUS IS only one part of our reconnecting with God. In Christian faith, the other side of the cross is resurrection. What we lose in following Jesus, we quickly learn to call the 'old' life, for he constantly gives us new life. We can be linked with the resurrection of Jesus in such a way that our lives are recreated. It is possible to access the vivifying power of one who died and then lived again.

The belief that Jesus rose from the dead after his crucifixion has been the cornerstone of Christian faith from the beginning. Jesus' disciples turned from an attitude of wilted defeat to one of energetic triumph three days after his death. Eyewitnesses to the wild news that Jesus lived again proclaimed their message with consistency and enthusiasm. Christianity spread like a brush fire. Its fuel was the resurrection.

The New Testament records further reflection on the meaning of Jesus' living again. The early Christians believed it to be God's victory over death and the powers of evil for all time. The resurrection assured the ultimate ascendancy of God's love over our sin. Moreover, such new life could now be active in every follower of Christ. The disciples reported transformation in people throughout the world as a result of Jesus' resurrection.

Difficult to Believe

But if the meaning of the death of Jesus has been a problem for people these days, the resurrection is even more so. The church still makes a big splash at Easter, but rarely speaks of resurrection power the rest of the year. Many of us in the church have lost the ability to wield the great energy of resurrection in our daily struggles.

The whole idea of someone rising from the dead makes little sense. It's a fun notion, but such things just don't happen. Many of us are not inclined to believe it. And even if we do believe in Jesus' resurrection, we haven't a clue as to how that affects us now.

We are in a perilous place with the resurrection. Interacting with Jesus through stories that are two thousand years old depends on his still being alive and active in the world. Christianity claims that there is real power for overcoming the real grip of evil in the world. We describe the symptoms of such evil these days as dysfunction, addiction, control needs, depression, and manipulation. Something greater than we are is needed to escape their power. Christianity succeeds or fails on the resurrection. If Jesus rose, then tremendous power for new life is available. If he did not, we are left with some good stories, and a decent ethic for compassion, but no real hope for ever living out the healing and the love credited to Jesus. And many, many Christians can no longer find the truth of the resurrection. They are groping for it as one might search for the dropped pair of glasses in the dark. I can't see to find my glasses without the light on; I can't find the light without my glasses; I am reduced to stumbling blindly.

All along, we have been exploring ways back into a relationship with Jesus for those who have felt on the outside of Christian faith. The resurrection is the most difficult story of all to grasp from the outside. But fortunately, the Gospel of Luke has recorded a story of two disciples who left their insider positions with the rest of Jesus' followers. On Easter Sunday they did not stay with everyone else. They were heading away from Jerusalem and the first bewildering reports of Jesus' missing body. These two did not apprehend the news of the resurrection; it seemed impossible, and so they left town, still sad and confused.

All of the disciples had been in the city of Jerusalem during the time of Jesus' trial and death. They had stayed together during the next two days, trying to figure out what to do next.

On Sunday afternoon, two of them struck out for a village called Emmaus, about seven miles from the city. As they walked, they discussed all the details of recent days, just as people who have experienced critical events need to go over and over every moment.

Perhaps they felt that if they just talked about it enough, some sense could be made.

The story tells us that Jesus drew up alongside them, but the disciples did not recognize him. 'What are you discussing?' he asked them. The two men stopped walking; sadness showed in their faces. It is one thing to go over the story with someone who has been through it with you; it's another thing to have to bring someone else up to date on the terrible events.

'Are you the only stranger in Jerusalem who does not know the things that have taken place there in these days?' said one of them.

'What things?' Jesus asked them.

And then the two went on to tell him the story from their point of view:

The things about Jesus of Nazareth, who was a prophet mighty in deed and word before God and all the people, and how our chief priests and leaders handed him over to be condemned to death and crucified him. But we had hoped that he was the one to redeem Israel. Yes, and besides all this, it is now the third day since these things took place. Moreover, some women of our group astounded us. They were at the tomb early this morning, and when they did not find his body there, they came back and told us that they had indeed seen a vision of angels who said that he was alive. Some of those who were with us went to the tomb and found it just as the women had said; but they did not see him.

Luke 24:19–24

These two men, if they were with us today, would have been outside on the sidewalk in front of the church filled with lilies and the choir's 'Hallelujah Chorus', talking about whether it was worth going inside. All the pieces for resurrection were in place, but they could not grasp it. They remained sad over Jesus' death. The possibility of his rising again did not grab hold in their minds.

I wonder how this sounded to Jesus as he walked next to them. He had told them he would be put to death and that he would rise. The women had found the tomb empty; angels had spoken to them. The disciples had all the clues but they could not solve the puzzle. It just did not make sense.

'Oh, how foolish you are, and how slow of heart to believe,' Jesus said, though this rebuke did not seem to register. A fog was over their minds. The reality of resurrection eluded them. Jesus went on to recount for them all the passages of scripture which spoke of the Christ. He went through them step by step to show how they all pointed to him. He was the Christ; he was the messiah who had to suffer first, then triumph. Along those seven miles, the two disciples received a Bible study from Jesus himself about what his life and death and rising meant.

As they arrived in Emmaus, Jesus acted as if he were continuing on his journey. The two other men begged him to stay the night with them. Jesus agreed. That night, at supper, Jesus took a loaf of bread, gave thanks, and then broke it to be passed among them. In that moment, they recognized him at last. Then he vanished from their sight. The disciples started talking, 'Were not our hearts burning within us while he was talking to us on the road, while he was opening the scriptures to us?'

Immediately, they hurried back to Jerusalem to report to the others.

Burning Hearts

The essence of this story seems to be about discerning the truth of the resurrection. All the clues may be at hand, but something critical is needed for our eyes actually to see what is before us. Perhaps the essential ingredient is the burning heart.

In the Old Testament, we can find the image of the burning heart first appearing in the book of Jeremiah. The prophet had reached a point where he no longer wanted to preach the word of God to the people of Israel. He was tired of being ridiculed for his warnings. So he tried to quit. Jeremiah wanted to live as if God did not really speak to him. But he found that the burning in his heart made the reality of God undeniably vivid for him. He wrote:

> So the word of the Lord has brought me
> insult
> and reproach all day long.
> But if I say, 'I will not mention him
> or speak any more
> in his name,'

his word is in my heart like a fire,
  a fire shut up in my bones.
I am weary of holding it in;
  indeed, I cannot.

Jeremiah 20:8b–9 (NIV)

Jeremiah's account makes me imagine something inside that must come out and find expression. The burning heart is a sign of incompletion demanding to be made whole; something within that will not rest until its outer complement is achieved. God sets the heart burning within and the fire cannot be quenched until some word is spoken, some deed done, or understanding grasped. When the heart burns, it is a sign that we are on to something important.

The burning heart is a phrase which evokes for me a feeling of being deeply moved. With this image I feel on the verge of experiencing something wonderful. Some great understanding is on the edge of the mind, and the heart burns to gain it. Our noses burn before the wonderful release of a sneeze. Our hearts may burn before the release of experiencing something new for which we have been longing. The phrase makes me feel a full heart, much energy and expectation; the burning heart is aflame with hope and desire.

A man rising from the dead can seem rationally impossible; we struggle to apprehend the meaning of such a claim because we have no direct comparisons in our experience. It is difficult to find an entry point. Perhaps, though, we can grasp something larger by grasping something on a smaller scale which points the way to the truth of the greater event. If we can identify moments of the burning heart, perhaps they can lead us to the resurrection.

If we can notice the places where our hearts begin to crackle with kindling flames, then perhaps we can stoke the fires and apprehend Jesus' rising.

Stoking the Fire

In our story, the resurrected Jesus was known in two indirect ways: in the discussion of the scriptures and in the breaking of bread. Along the way Jesus recalled many passages and shared their meaning. That was when the disciples' hearts burned. I hope that your heart has burned from time to time in reading the Gospel stories we have studied. When Scripture grabs hold of us, we may feel that we have been known; our lives have been named in God's presence. And then we are swept up in the power of God's reality.

There are some passages in the New Testament which kindle flames in my heart by suggesting that our lives may be linked to the resurrection of Jesus. Two from the letters of Paul to the churches are particularly evocative:

> Since, then, you have been raised with Christ, set your hearts on things above, where Christ is seated at the right hand of God.
>
> Colossians 3:1 (NIV)

> Therefore we have been buried with him by baptism into death, so that, just as Christ was raised from the dead by the glory of the Father, we too might walk in newness of life. For if we have been united with him in a death like his, we will certainly be united with him in a resurrection like his.
>
> Romans 6:4–5

These verses seem to be an encouragement to imagine ourselves as participants in the resurrection. We may 'walk in newness of life' because Jesus is raised. The fact that 'you have been raised with Christ' forms the basis for a new way of living. Now we may set our hearts 'on things above.'

I invite you to take these verses as your own. Say aloud, 'I have been raised with Christ. I will set my heart on things above, where Christ is. Because Jesus was raised from the dead, I may walk in newness of life today. One day, after I die, I will live again with Christ.' Does that begin to kindle your soul?

There are other areas of life where we may identify the burning heart and allow it to direct us to the truth of the resurrection. Going outdoors alone, to walk or sit in such a way that we receive what is before us can often spark us. It takes effort to set aside other agendas; it can be painful to be still for a change. But such labour can release imagination and energy.

Can you remember watching clouds move across the sky? Animal shapes appeared, then re-formed into other creatures. Perhaps there was an afternoon when you looked long enough for it to seem as if the world was moving, not the clouds. The house seemed to be falling forwards while the clouds stayed still. Years later, one spring day, you may walk outside, notice the clouds moving, and be struck. A spark of memory catches in your heart. This is important; if I could just slow down enough to look, my heart is burning for this moment.

Sometimes our hearts burn when we look at children. Those with children in their homes may recall walking into the kitchen one afternoon to find the three-year-old who was supposed to be taking a nap, sitting on the counter. He has pulled a chair over from the table and used it as a ladder. Then he got down a mixing bowl and proceeded to put everything sweet, spicy, gooey, and runny from the cupboard into the bowl. Half of it is on his face, the other half is on the counter and floor. Just for a second, the flame in your heart kindles. Isn't this wonderful! He's so resourceful; he's so funny. The little guy loves his life and the mess he has made.

The heart burns and it tells us something about life, but just for a second. The flame retardant of our need to clean up gets sprayed everywhere. Look at this mess! What have you done? What has he done but interrupt the day with the flame of life's joy that leads to seeing the resurrected Christ, if we don't quench it too soon.

In an argument, the heart may burn. You go back and forth with someone you love over some trivial issue. You duel it out over nothing. And then, your heart flickers with a thought, 'I'm not really interested in this argument. I'm just fighting because I can't stop. Really, I don't want to hurt her; I just want to be near her.' For that moment you are aware of the burning flame of how life could be. You could call a halt; swallow pride; not say the ugly thing. You could live in a new way. There is a moment of choice, usually unrecognized, when we can refrain from the harmful word. The heart burns with the things from above.

There is no proof for the resurrection that entirely satisfies our doubts. Even if all our criteria for belief were answered, it would not be enough. Some experience of the burning heart is needed. Where could I send you for that? I could not guarantee any miracle or vision. No voice in the night or secret knowledge can be promised. I could, though, suggest that the answer is near at hand, closer than we ever thought, if we could just dislodge ourselves from daily busyness to see it.

I could ask you to go away for a couple of days, if you are really serious about this, and discover what it is you miss. Go away but do not be too busy, too distracted. Leave time and room for your heart to do its work. Get away to feel again what you love. And ponder the mystery once you have felt it. Why is there a hole in my life when I am away from that one or that place or those people? There, in the mystery of love, you might feel the presence of God which kindles the heart and answers doubt.

I could ask you to go out in the yard or the woods and put your hands in the earth. Stoop down and look at a wild flower: not in the soupy 'Oh, isn't it lovely' kind of way; look in a way that is still and painful and time consuming. Count the petals; name the colours; articulate the shape.

Consider how year after year the flower returns to live for just a few weeks, then is gone. What purpose does it have but beauty in itself. Whether anyone sees it or not, the flower simply is itself and is beautiful. There, in the mystery of the world, your heart might be set to burning, and the resurrection might be experienced as true.

And there is one more way to consider. In our story, the disciples recognized Jesus when during supper he broke the bread and gave it to them. Illumination was created when a ritual was enacted that reminded them of the Last Supper. They shared an activity which evoked a common memory. And they shared a common meaning of the moment: Jesus said he was giving himself to us in the bread and the cup; here is the bread, and look, here is Jesus! The traditional symbols of Christian faith can have a renewed power in our lives as we approach them freshly. One way into the resurrection is the obvious one. We may find the risen Jesus in worship and communion.

Further, the way the disciples recognized Jesus tells us how much we need each other. Ultimately, it is up to God to illumine the truth of the resurrection for us. Jesus is the one who lifted the fog from his followers' eyes. But the recognition came in the context of the disciples' conversation during their journey, of their considering together the scriptures Jesus recited, and of their being together at the table. We need one another to help us recall the stories which set our hearts burning. Others are necessary companions for discussing and processing all the events of our lives as we make our way along the road. And we need each other to learn how to wield the signs and symbols of faith. We even need each other to help get us to church and study groups. Many aspects of reconnecting to God have to be done in solitude, but we never get very far without others to keep us going.

The Power of the Resurrection

The power of Jesus' resurrection for us lies in the fact that Jesus' followers are mystically linked to both his dying and his rising. We may access the great energy of Jesus' resurrection in our own lives. The first step is to identify with the death, as we have seen in many ways throughout this book. Then we may set our hearts on the things above and walk in newness of life.

In his book, *Dreams*, Morton Kelsey has written, 'Since Jesus has risen from the dead, there is no power He cannot overcome.' Throughout this study we have explored the great energy for life that Jesus had. His stories revealed the resurrecting quality of God's all-forgiving love for us. The father told the prodigal, 'This son of mine was dead and is alive again; he was lost and is found!' In his personal encounters, Jesus offered the clarity of living water to the woman at the well, and a new start to the weeping woman plagued by her past. He had the strength to show a deeper way to the rich man, and the courage to bend down to wash his disciples' feet. In all his interactions, Jesus offered to free people from old, lifeless ways and to guide them into the vivid life of following him. The beginning always meant a kind of death; the ending, for those who passed through the first stage, always meant a kind of resurrection.

By now I am hopeful that you number yourself as one of Jesus' followers. We can be linked to his resurrection. We have a new life. The Spirit of God is within us. We have risen with Christ. This is our heritage as Christians. We may claim it, lean upon it, and revel in it at any time.

Questions for Reflection and Discussion

The story of the disciples' walk to Emmaus is found in Luke 24:13–35.

1) What questions or difficulties have you had about the resurrection?

2) What kept the disciples from recognizing Jesus?

3) Why was the breaking of the bread the moment of illumination for them?

4) What do you think the disciples meant when they said, 'Were not our hearts burning within us while he was talking to us on the road, while he was opening the scriptures to us?'

5) What does the phrase 'burning heart' evoke for you? When have you felt your heart burn? What followed the sensation?

6) Have there been moments of resurrection in your life? Have there been moments of really believing or feeling Jesus' resurrection?

Exercises

1) Individually, work on a dialogue in which you join the other two disciples along the Emmaus road and speak to Jesus about his life, death, and resurrection. Allow your questions to surface, and allow his replies to arise through answers or actions.

2) If you are working with a group, after writing the dialogues, hold a group dialogue in which you discuss the meaning of Jesus' resurrection, your experiences of resurrection, and any insights you gained from your writing.

3) Meditate on this prayer from the 1979 *Book of Common Prayer*:

> Lord Jesus, stay with us, for the evening is at hand and the day is past; be our companion in the way, kindle our hearts, and awaken hope, that we may know thee as thou art revealed in Scripture and the breaking of bread. Grant this for the sake of thy love. Amen.

~11~

Heartfelt

O UR FINAL STORY TOOK PLACE AFTER THE resurrection. Simon Peter and some of the other disciples had gone fishing. Once long ago they had fished all night and caught nothing, until Jesus sent them out for the miraculous catch. This night as well, their fishing had left them empty-handed.

At dawn, they saw a man standing on the beach. He called to them, 'Children, you have no fish, have you?' When they replied that they did not, he suggested, 'Cast the net to the right side of the boat, and you will find some.' And then there were so many fish that they could not haul the net aboard.

A flash of *déjà vu* went through John. 'It is the Lord!' When Simon Peter realized the man on the shore was the resurrected Jesus, he leaped into the water and swam to him. Jesus was cooking fish over a charcoal fire.

'Come and have breakfast,' Jesus said to them. And he took a loaf of bread, broke it, and gave it to the disciples. Again the feeling of *déjà vu* passed through them. Here was the Last Supper and the dinner at Emmaus all over again. Jesus passed out the fish as well, and the disciples ate breakfast with their master who had returned from the dead.

After breakfast, Jesus turned to Simon. 'Simon son of John, do you love me more than these?'

Simon replied immediately, 'Yes, Lord; you know that I love you.'

And just as quickly Jesus added, 'Feed my lambs.' Then he asked again, 'Simon son of John, do you love me?' After a similar exchange, Jesus asked still another time if Simon loved him. The text tells us that Simon was hurt that Jesus had to keep asking.

He answered emphatically, 'Lord, you know everything; you know that I love you.' And Jesus simply said, 'Feed my sheep.'

We have seen the use of repetition in the story of the foot washing and in the parable of the sheep and goats. Once again, the importance Jesus placed on his question is unmistakable. He wanted much more than a casual, immediate response. Jesus required Simon Peter to answer from his depths. The obvious reason for the repetition is that Peter had denied knowing Jesus three times on the night before the crucifixion. Here was an opportunity for

Peter to proclaim his love three times and be reinstated. But perhaps there is even more to it, in some dimension that affects us.

Do You Love Me?

'Do you love Jesus?' The question is so straightforward as to be unnerving. One might reply, 'Well, I don't know. I mean I guess so. I don't *not* love Jesus. I want to follow him. Sure, all right, then, I love him.' The first time the issue is raised, we might be able to stumble through and then forget about it.

But what if Jesus himself were to ask the question the second time, and call us by name when he asked, 'Do you love me?' I begin to get uncomfortable. Is there something the matter? Don't you believe me when I say I love you? You are making me doubt myself. You are embarrassing me.

And if he were to ask the question still a third time, we might begin to realize how earnestly he desires our reply. He really does hope we will be bold enough to express our love. But he will not accept a superficial answer. It has to come from deep within; it has to mean everything. He is demanding that we become conscious of our disposition toward him. Simply plodding along not thinking about him will not do. The question is repeated until we are awake enough to make a true answer. Jesus is relentless in this questioning, and behind his queries is his love for us that is equally relentless. He loves us ardently; he has a work for us to do in the world, and he wants to know our response.

How would you reply? The answer could be 'I don't know right now. I am not sure I know enough yet.' And then I must consider how I want to express that ambivalence. Do I want to say, 'No I don't love you. I do not, I will not love Jesus'? And if I am bold enough to articulate such a reply, then I will consider if that is the direction I want my life to take. Will I consciously live with the choice of not loving him?

By contrast, do I want to say 'Yes, of course I love you'? Or if that is too bold for my hesitant faith, do I want *to want* to love Jesus? Is there some kernel, some tiny irreducible part of me that is yearning to love Christ and express that love? Then I will consider how I can work with that nugget of hope and fan it into a more ardent love.

An Evening of Discovery

Blaise Pascal was a French mathematician and scientist who lived in the seventeenth century. As a young man, he had a deeply religious nature, but was not satisfied with the depth of his relationship with God. On a November night in 1654, at the age of thirty-one, Pascal had what he described as a second conversion experience. Suddenly he saw the reality of God which undergirded all the mathematics of the universe. The period of two hours was visionary and awoke his love for Christ. When it was over, Pascal recorded his experience and kept it with him at all times as the touchstone of his life. This excerpt is deeply moving to me:

> The year of grace 1654,
> Monday, 23 November, Feast of Saint
>   Clement, Pope and Martyr...
> From about half-past-ten in the evening
>   until half-past-midnight
> FIRE
> 'God of Abraham, God of Isaac, God of
>   Jacob,' not of philosophers and
>   scholars,
> Certainty, certainty, heartfelt, joy, peace.
> God of Jesus Christ.
> God of Jesus Christ.
> 'My God and your God,'
> 'Thy God shall be my God.'
> The world forgotten, and everything
>   except God.
> He can only be found by the ways

taught in the Gospels.

Greatness of the human soul.

'O righteous Father, the world had not
    known thee, but I have known thee.'

Joy, joy, joy, tears of joy.

I have cut myself off from him.

'They have forsaken me, the fountain of
    living waters.'

My God wilt thou forsake me?

Let me not be cut off from him for ever!

'And this is life eternal, that they might
    know thee, the only true God, and
    Jesus Christ whom thou hast sent.'

Jesus Christ.

Jesus Christ... [1]

If you have not already, I invite you to read
this passage aloud several times. I feel in its language a great sense of illumination; Pascal moved
to a new place in his life. Suddenly he discerned
the reality of God and his love was awakened. All
his studies had been fascinating but were not a sufficient end in themselves. His brilliant, rational
mind gave way to the sense of his heart. What he
knew now was more than rational. 'Certainty, certainty, **heartfelt**, joy, peace.' Pascal's response to
what God had revealed to him arose from the centre of his heart.[2]

The time comes when we have interacted with Jesus enough to find ourselves in active relationship with him. And if we are blessed, this awareness of how important Jesus is to our very being gives rise to a great outpouring of love. After being blocked from God for so long, we see our floodgates open. We can express our love.

Though You Have Not Seen Him

I imagine that this final episode with Jesus had a lasting effect on Simon Peter. In a letter he dictated years later, he wrote this about the follower's relationship with Jesus: 'Although you have not seen him [Jesus], you love him; and even though you do not see him now, you believe in him and rejoice with an indescribable and glorious joy, for you are receiving the outcome of your faith, the salvation of your souls' (1 Peter 1:8–9).

Peter wrote to people he had never met and told them that they loved Jesus and believed in him. I remember the afternoon I read this passage and wondered, 'How do you know that I love him? You don't know anything about me. I don't even know myself if I love Christ or not.' And then, as if in direct response to my unspoken question, these words of Simon Peter seemed to lift me to a higher plane. I suddenly felt that I did not need to keep questioning myself about whether I felt enough or believed strongly enough or was at the right place spiritually. I did not have to try to reconnect with God; there was nothing to search for. The words of this passage brought me to the place I had longed to be.

A wave of relief hit me. 'All right', I thought, 'I do love him. I don't have to pick at these introspective worries any more. Peter says I believe, and I'll agree with that. I do believe. I really do love Jesus. I am, by God's grace, already connected.'

There followed 'an indescribable and glorious joy.' Certainty, not intellectual but heartfelt. Closeness, not by my striving but as a gift. All I had to do was agree with what was declared about me. Though I have not seen him, I love him.

Feed My Lambs

Each time that Simon Peter answered Jesus in the affirmative, Christ responded, 'Feed my lambs. Tend my sheep.' Jesus wanted Peter to experience and express confidence in his devotion. But that was not to be the end of it. The internal 'Yes' required an outer expression. Peter's life was not just about the discovery of his own fulfilment in a relationship with Christ. There was work to be done. The lambs needed to be fed and the sheep tended.

We begin the journey of reconnecting to God because of our own needs. We find ourselves penniless and far from home, and our hunger sends us on the way. We find ourselves so thirsty that we finally have to ask for a drink when our water supply no longer satisfies. Our accumulation of wealth does not fulfil us and before we know it we are asking, 'What must I do to inherit eternal life?' The weight of life can steal upon us so quickly that even before we know it, we are weeping at Jesus' feet. Our first steps arise out of our need, and that is perfectly fine. We were made to be in a relationship with God. Reconnecting is the necessary beginning point of our new lives.

But in the larger purposes of God, we do not follow Jesus just for our own sakes. God wants to bring the whole creation the healing, restoring love that Jesus gave to people. And for some unfathomable reason, God has chosen human beings to be the heralds of that love. Others are waiting for us to reconnect with God so that we may bring God's tender mercies to them.

If this were just about my spiritual comfort or lack of it, I could justify piddling around for years. I'll be miserable if I want to be, thank you very much. But the heart of God is aching for our return.

And the little ones whom Jesus loved so much are waiting for us to go to them. For our sake, we need to follow Jesus, and also for the sake of those to whom we are sent.

At the end of this study, I find that the query of Jesus is still piercingly clear: 'Do you love me more than these?' More than all the other ways I have tried living. More than all the distractions I cherish. More than the pain I nurse. And sometimes, even in spite of myself, my soul answers for me, 'Lord, you know that I love you.' The response is more than rational; it is heartfelt. And so his call is clarion, 'Then feed my lambs.'

Questions for Reflection and Discussion

The story of the breakfast on the beach is in John 21:1–19.

1) Why might Simon Peter have gone fishing that night? In what ways do we try to go back to the familiar life after we have experienced a taste of the resurrection? What happens?

2) What do you imagine Simon Peter felt when Jesus asked him the question the first time, 'Do you love me?' How about the second and third times?

3) How would you respond if Jesus asked you if you loved him?

4) How does it feel to you to hear Peter's affirmation: 'Although you have not seen him, you love him; and even though you do not see him now, you believe in him'?

5) Who are the lambs and sheep you suspect Jesus may want you to tend and feed?

Exercises

1) Pretend that you are Simon Peter later that night, reflecting on what happened on the beach. Write a paragraph expressing what you think Jesus was after by his questions, what you think he may want you to do, and how you are feeling since the encounter.

2) Spend an entire day assuming that you do believe in Jesus, that you do love him enough to want to follow him, and that you will feed his sheep. For the whole day, pretending if you need to, verbalize that affirmation and live as if it were so. In the evening write a reflection on how it felt to assume such a connection with God.

Did your 'trying out' of that relationship enable you in any way to realize that you are already connected with God?

3) For a prayer, use the Pascal quotation from earlier in the chapter.

Notes

[1] From George Appleton, editor, *The Oxford Book of Prayer*, Oxford University Press, New York, 1985, pages 264–265.

[2] It is interesting to note that after such an awareness of God's presence, Pascal was struck with a sense of his unworthiness ('I have cut myself off from him') much like what Simon and Isaiah experienced in the passages we studied in Chapter 4. His simple uttering of 'Jesus Christ / Jesus Christ' indicates God's response of grace to Pascal's confession.

Acknowledgments

The publisher gratefully acknowledges permission to reprint the following excerpts:

'Christmas Poor', 'Thou Art God' and the excerpt from 'The Hymn of St Patrick' from *The Edge of Glory* by David Adam. Used by kind permission of Triangle/SPCK, London.

Excerpts from *The Divine Liturgy According to St John Chrysostom* used by permission of St Tikhon's Seminary Press, South Canaan, PA 18459.

Excerpts from 'East Coker', 'Little Gidding', and 'The Dry Salvages' in *Four Quartets*, copyright © 1943 by T.S. Eliot and renewed 1971 by Esme Valerie Eliot, reprinted by permission of Harcourt Brace & Company and Faber & Faber, Ltd.

Excerpt from *Markings* by Dag Hammarskjöld, translated by Leif Sjöberg and W.H. Auden. Translation copyright © by Alfred A. Knopf, Inc. and Faber & Faber, Ltd. Reprinted by permission of Alfred A. Knopf, Inc. and Faber & Faber, Ltd.

If you have enjoyed reading *Heartfelt*, you may wish to know that BRF produces two regular series of Bible reading notes published three times a year (in January, May and September). *Guidelines* contains commentary and reflection on the Bible, arranged in weekly sections, with a devotional 'Guidelines' section each week. *New Daylight* contains daily readings with printed Bible passages, brief comments and prayers, and is also available in a large print version.

Copies of *New Daylight* and *Guidelines* may be obtained from your local Christian bookshop or by subscription direct from BRF (see over).

For more information about *New Daylight*, *Guidelines* and the full range of BRF publications, write to: The Bible Reading Fellowship, Peter's Way, Sandy Lane West, OXFORD OX4 5HG (Tel. 01865 748227)

SUBSCRIPTION ORDER FORM

Please send me the following, beginning with the Jan/May/Sep* issue:

Qty   £

____ Guidelines   £9.00 p.a.   _____

____ New Daylight   £9.00 p.a.   _____

____ New Daylight large print   £12.00 p.a.   _____

*delete as appropriate

All prices include postage and packing.

Please complete the payment details below—all orders must be accompanied by the appropriate payment—and send your completed order to **BRF, Peter's Way, Sandy Lane West, Oxford OX4 5HG.**

Name . . . .

Address . . . .

. . . . Postcode . . . .

Signed. . . . . Date . . . .

Payment for subscription(s)   £ _____
Donation   £ _____
Total enclosed   £ _____

Payment by cheque □ postal order □ Visa □ Mastercard □

Expiry date of card . . . .

Signature . . . .

(essential if paying by credit card)

BRF is a Reg. Charity (No. 233280)   HF

NB *New Daylight* and *Guidelines* may also be obtained from your local Christian bookshop—ask at your local shop for details.